The Room Goes Quiet: How to Close High-Stakes Service Deals by Owning Customer Risk

William Anderson

The Room Goes Quiet: How to Close High-Stakes Service Deals by Owning Customer Risk

William Anderson

Cover Art from Willian Anderson

The Room Goes Quiet: How to Close High-Stakes Service Deals by Owning Customer Risk by William Anderson

This edition published in 2026

Published by Winged Hussar Publishing, LLC
Iron Strategy Press
1525 Hulse Road, Unit 1
Point Pleasant, NJ 08742

HC ISBN 978-1-958872-93-2
EB ISBN 978-1-958872-94-9
LCN

Bibliographical References and Index
1. Business. 2. Sales. 3. Help

copyright © William Anderon 2026

For more information on Winged Hussar Publishing, LLC, visit us at:
https://www.whpsupplyroom.com

This book is sold subject to the condition that it shall not, by way of trade or otherwise, be lent, resold, hired out, or otherwise circulated without the publisher's prior consent in any form of binding or cover other than that in which it is published and without a similar condition, including this condition, being imposed on the subsequent purchaser.

All rights reserved. No part of this book may be reproduced, stored in a retrieval system, or transmitted in any form or by any means - electronic, mechanical, photocopying, recording, or otherwise - without the prior written permission of the publisher, except in the case of brief quotations used in reviews or scholarly works. This book is for informational and educational purposes only. The author and publisher make no representations or warranties regarding the accuracy, applicability, or completeness of the contents.

Table of Contents

Introduction: This Isn't a Sales Book 6

Part I: Foundation—The Strategic Service Sales Mindset 7
    Chapter 1: The New Reality of Service Sales 8
        Case Study: The Deal That Was Lost in 45 Minutes 15
    Chapter 2: Integrity in Sales – The Foundation of Lasting Success 19
    Chapter 3: The Psychology of B2B Buying – Navigating Fear, Confidence, and Risk in Sales 26
        Case Study: Trust Wins Deals 31
    Chapter 4: The Strategic Partnership Framework – Moving Beyond Traditional Service Sales 35
        Case Study: How Trust, Clarity, and Risk Ownership Won the Deal 39
    Chapter 5: From Insight to Execution – What Comes Next Isn't Theory 44

Part II: Building Trust Through Strategic Alignment 47
    Chapter 6: Who Really Sells the Work? 48
    Chapter 7: The Service Seller Archetypes 50
    Chapter 8: Modern Models – When Services Are the Reason Deals Succeed ... 56
    Chapter 9: Understanding Customer Behavior & Strategic Empathy in Service Sales 62
        Case Study: Tactical Empathy in Action 69
    Chapter 10: The Silent Advantage – Mastering Body Language & Non-Verbal Sales Cues 73
    Chapter 11: Taking Responsibility for Customer Outcomes 78
        Case Study: The Power of a Well-Timed Success Story 82
    Chapter 12: Reframing Risk – Turning Buyer Hesitation into Forward Motion 86
    Chapter 13: The Risk Ownership Framework: Four Pillars of Service Sales 90

Part III: Execution—From Strategy to Success 93
    Chapter 14: Qualifying Opportunities Through Collaboration & Strategic Positioning 94
        Case Study: The Champion Who Wasn't a Decision-Maker 100
    Chapter 15: Risk Management & Deal Governance – From Mitigation to Strategic Advantage 106
    Chapter 16: Value Translation – When Numbers Tell the Story 113
    Chapter 17: Turning Conversations into Commitments 119
        Case Study: From Bottleneck to Breakthrough 123
    Chapter 18: From Value to Commitment 129
        Case Study: Ten Seconds of Silence 137
    Chapter 19: Selling the Long-Term Vision 140
    Chapter 20: Unsticking a Deal – Turning Stagnation into Momentum 144
    Chapter 21: Winning When You're Not There 147
        Case Study: The Fortune 500 Procurement Trap 150
        Case Study: The $50,000 Discount That Should Never Have Happened 156
        Case Study: The Multimillion-Dollar Deal Saved by a Strategic Risk Discussion 161
    Chapter 22: Mastering Procurement – Winning Against Cost-Centric Buyers .. 167

Chapter 23: Scaling Execution into Repeatable Success 172

Part IV: Scale—Building Sustainable Success **173**
    Chapter 24: Scaling Service Sales Without Losing Strategic Value 174
        Case Study: The "Just Do It Internally" Deal Saved by Mentor-Based Approach 181
    Chapter 25: From Sales to Execution – Building Trust at Every Step 186
        Case Study: Breaking the Growth Ceiling 192
    Chapter 26: When the Room Stays Quiet: Resilience and Identity as a Service Seller 195
    Chapter 27: Preparing for the Future of Service Sales 199
    Chapter 28: Adapting the Framework for Scalable, Sustainable Service Sales 201

Part V: The Future of Service Sales—Adapting to a Changing Landscape **207**
    Chapter 29: The Future of Service Sales 208
    Chapter 30: The Limits of AI in Service Sales – Where Humans Still Win ... 213
    Chapter 31: The Augmented Seller: Using AI Without Losing Trust 218
    Chapter 32: Adapting Services Sales to Modern Revenue Recognition Models 221
        Case Study: The Sales Rep, the Spreadsheet, and the RevRec Reckoning 226
    Chapter 33: The Margin Mindset – Why Sales Must Care About Profitability 229
    Chapter 34: Protecting Margin in the Field – Pricing, Scope & Delivery Strategy 233
    Chapter 35: Margin as Strategy – Executive Levers for Scalable Profitability ... 238
        Case Study: Margin Discipline in the Field: Two Paths, Two Outcomes 243
    Chapter 36: The High Cost of Chasing the Clock 248
    Chapter 37: The Future of Service Sales – Adapting to a Changing Landscape 253

When the Room Goes Quiet **255**

Appendix: Tools, Frameworks, and Execution Models **257**

Authors Note **264**

About the Author **266**

Introduction: This Isn't a Sales Book

This is a book for people who sell what others are afraid to own.

If you're in consulting, professional services, or solution delivery—this isn't optional reading. This is the missing manual. Because you're not selling licenses or features or widgets. You're selling conviction. You're selling execution. You're selling the belief that when the pressure's on, *you're the one who shows up and gets it done*.

Most sales books don't apply to your world. They're written for product sellers playing a different game: high volume, quick wins, and minimal fallout. That's not your reality. In services, you're often walking into a deal where the customer has *already failed once*, is out of political capital, and is one mistake away from being replaced. And they want to know: *Can I trust you to carry this risk with me?*

This book is built for that moment.

It's not theory. It's not fluff. It's a field manual for professionals who sell complex, high-risk solutions and who are still standing when everyone else steps back. It's for those who win trust not through pressure or pricing games, but through presence, ownership, and clarity in the moments that matter.

You won't find gimmicks on these pages. You'll find stories, tactics, and playbooks born from real deals, real friction, and real outcomes. If you've ever walked into a customer meeting and felt the weight of what happens if you fail—this book is for you.

Let's begin with one of those moments.

William Anderson

Part I: Foundation—The Strategic Service Sales Mindset

Chapter 1: The New Reality of Service Sales

A twenty-million-dollar deal was lost in forty-five minutes—not because of price, not because of capability, but because the service provider couldn't answer one question:

"What happens if we fail?"

The room fell silent. The executive team, once engaged, leaned back in their chairs. Arms crossed. Expressions are neutral but no longer open. In that moment, the dynamic shifted. They weren't looking for a vendor with good intentions. They were searching for a strategic partner who could carry weight. Someone who understood what was really at stake.

Instead, what they heard was uncertainty.

They didn't walk away because the provider lacked expertise. They walked away because the provider failed to take ownership. They couldn't confidently say, "Here's how we manage failure. Here's how we protect your business, your team, your outcomes."

Within the hour, the deal was dead.

The competitor who won wasn't cheaper. They weren't more technically advanced. They simply removed doubt. They stepped in, took responsibility for results, and offered a clear path to success and recovery if needed. That was enough.

This is the new reality of service sales.

The High-Stakes Reality of Services

There was a time when service sales followed a familiar rhythm: build rapport, understand requirements, demo capabilities, submit a proposal, and negotiate on price. That rhythm still exists, but in high-stakes deals, it no longer closes.

Today's enterprise buyers don't just evaluate capability. They assess consequences. They ask, "If this fails, who absorbs the impact? Who's going to protect my credibility?" The seller who provides the clearest, most confident answer to that question wins.

What often looks like indecision or delay is actually something more calculating. Executives are weighing their exposure. They're evaluating not just what could go wrong, but who will stand with them if it does.

In this world, service sales isn't a process. It's a performance of credibility under pressure.

Why Traditional Sales Approaches Are Failing

A senior executive summed it up with quiet frustration during a strategy session:

"Ten years ago, service providers sold us expertise. Now everyone's got a slide deck and a certification. That doesn't move the needle anymore."

No one challenged him because he wasn't wrong. He wasn't rejecting services. He was rejecting the sameness of how they're sold.

The traditional model of sales, one built around education, credentials, and polished pitch decks, is breaking down. It assumes buyers are underinformed. It assumes that the right content will carry the day.

But buyers today are rarely uninformed. Often misinformed, sometimes overwhelmed, but not lacking access to knowledge. What they lack is clarity about whom they can trust when the stakes are high.

The Room Goes Quiet

Credentials don't close deals. Commitment does.

The Shift from Vendor to Strategic Partner

There is a clear and unmistakable line between being a vendor and being a partner:

- Vendors respond to requests. Partners anticipate needs.
- Vendors deliver what's asked. Partners co-create what's required.
- Vendors show up for the pitch. Partners show up for the risk.

In today's environment, that line matters more than ever.

When service providers all claim to "drive outcomes" and "partner for success," the language becomes meaningless. It's not that buyers don't value those claims. It's that they've heard them too many times without seeing them delivered.

In a sea of sameness, what stands out isn't the most polished presentation. It's the first moment a buyer feels real alignment, when they sense that the team across the table isn't reciting a script but carrying weight alongside them.

Here's how the distinction plays out:

Vendor	Strategic Partner
Respond to an RFP	Shapes the solution upstream
Focus on scope and Cost	Focus on risks and outcome
Waits for customer to define success	Co-defines what success means
Avoids accountability for failure	Plans for and owns recovery scenarios
Engages late in buying cycle	Engages early and influences decision
The goal isn't to get selected.	The goal is to be essential.

Expertise Isn't Enough Anymore

There was a time when certifications, frameworks, and reference logos could win the room. But buyers have been through too many cycles. They've heard the jargon. They've seen elegant strategies fall apart in real environments and bulletproof plans crack under pressure.

One buyer said it plainly: "Expertise doesn't mean anything if your team disappears after kickoff."

That's the heart of the problem. Traditional selling stops at proving capability. But today's buyer is really asking, "Who protects me when this gets hard?" It's not about intelligence. It's about presence and about durability under stress.

And it's about proving, not just claiming, that you'll show up when it counts.

The Rise of Sameness in the Age of AI

Review a few modern pitch decks and you'll see a pattern.

Slide one: "We understand your challenges"

Slide two: "Here's our methodology"

Slide three: "Why we're different"

Slide four: Capability matrix

Slide five: Case study cropped to fit a slide

It's clean. It's correct. And it's forgettable.

Because now even average providers can generate that narrative using AI. The structure is standard. The visuals are impressive. But the substance is hollow. Buyers can feel it. They know when something was crafted by an engineer or a marketing team versus when it comes from lived experience.

The Room Goes Quiet

What matters is not how clean your template looks, but how precisely you connect with the buyer's unspoken fears and internal constraints. You won't be trusted because you have a better slide. You'll be trusted because you say what no one else is saying—and mean it.

What wins now isn't polish. It's presence.

What Really Wins the Room

There's a turning point in every high-stakes sales conversation. It's not when the case study lands or when the pricing slide comes up.

It's when someone on your team names the risk that everyone else is avoiding. When they say, "If this doesn't land inside your environment, your culture, your resource model, none of it matters. So let's build it backward from that."

That moment shifts the entire room. In that moment, the buyer realizes you're not just selling. You're planning to carry weight with them.

You become the partner they didn't know how to ask for.

And once that shift happens, once you move from selling a solution to co-owning the outcome, the rest of the conversation isn't about closing. It's about alignment.

That's when real buying begins.

Execution Is the Proof of Partnership

Every service provider talks about outcomes. Every deck claims accountability. But intent is not enough.

Buyers aren't measuring what you say. They're measuring how you'll behave under pressure. They want to know what happens when conditions change, when internal support waivers, and when results take longer than expected.

What they're asking (whether or not they say it) is: "Will this partner make us stronger when things get tough?"

Answering that convincingly builds trust that survives procurement, politics, and setbacks.

Trust, not credentials, is the foundation of modern service sales.

This Is a Leadership Game Now

Service sales has evolved from being a technical sale to a leadership moment.

Buyers are no longer comparing vendors. They're comparing risk exposure. They're asking which team helps them avoid wasted time, reputational damage, or organizational backlash.

This evolution demands a new type of seller.

Not just someone with technical fluency, but someone with emotional range. Not just a confident presenter, but someone who listens for tension, reads the political undercurrents, and builds clarity across silos.

The sales team that wins the future isn't the one with the best demo. It's the one that redefines what safety feels like in a deal.

That starts with owning the customer's success before the contract is signed.

The Path Forward

So where does that leave us?

It leaves us at the beginning of a different kind of conversation. One not focused on persuasion, but on positioning. Not on perfecting the pitch, but on framing the problem in a way that causes buyers to say, "You're the one I trust to fix this."

The Room Goes Quiet

That's what the chapters ahead are built to do.

They'll walk through how to shift from selling services to owning outcomes. How to gain access earlier, shape executive priorities, manage internal politics, and earn trust that can't be automated or outbid.

Because once you make that shift and become the partner they bet on instead of the vendor they compare, the rules change.

Your access expands. Your pricing strengthens. Your influence deepens.

And the room doesn't just go quiet.

It turns your way.

William Anderson

Case Study: The Deal That Was Lost in 45 Minutes

The Setup: A Deal That Looked Like a Sure Win

For months, the sales team had nurtured this opportunity by shaping strategy sessions, guiding technical discovery, and building executive relationships. It was a $20 million services engagement with a global energy conglomerate, centered on full-scale infrastructure modernization and cloud migration.

The CIO was our champion. Procurement had pre-cleared the budget. The technical teams were aligned. The deal had been marked at 90 percent in every forecast for weeks.

Mike, the account executive, had been working on this pursuit for over a year. It was his signature opportunity. Lisa, the pre-sales consultant, had poured herself into it by architecting detailed solution diagrams, running multiday whiteboard sessions, and managing executive prep late into the night.

Everything was on track. The internal sentiment was celebratory. The final meeting with the customer's C-suite was seen not as a pitch but as a formality.

And that assumption cost us the deal.

The Moment It Fell Apart

The meeting started as expected. Mike walked through the roadmap. Lisa covered methodology and value realization. The CIO nodded approvingly. The COO asked sharp but friendly questions. The team felt in sync.

Then the CFO, who had been quiet throughout, leaned in. His fingers steepled. His tone direct:

"This looks good on paper. But what happens if this fails?"

The Room Goes Quiet

Silence.

The CIO, our most vocal supporter, suddenly looked down, and the COO leaned back and crossed his arms. The tension was immediate and palpable.

Lisa responded first, voice steady but rushed. "We've done this before; our model is proven. We've executed this transformation with companies in your space. Our references are strong."

The CFO didn't blink. "That's not what I asked."

Lisa faltered. Mike stepped in, offering process frameworks, escalation paths, and structured risk reviews.

"We adapt quickly. We monitor. If there's an issue, we correct before it becomes a problem. We have contingencies and checkpoints built in . . ."

But he never answered the question.

What happens if this fails?

The CFO wasn't looking for optimism. He was looking for ownership.

And what he heard was avoidance.

The meeting ran another fifteen minutes, but the energy had shifted. They stopped taking notes. Their questions became perfunctory. The room was already closing.

We walked in as the front-runners. We walked out as just another vendor.

The Competitor's Winning Move
When the loss was confirmed a week later, the CIO was candid.

- 16 -

"The other team answered the question."

They didn't offer a perfect plan. They didn't present a cheaper proposal. But when the CFO asked what happens if it all goes sideways, they didn't deflect.

They confronted the question head-on.

"Here's how this could fail. And here's what we do if it does."

That moment didn't just change the deal. It sealed it.

The CFO didn't want guarantees. He wanted to be confident that if the initiative faltered, he wouldn't be left to hold the blame alone.

He needed a partner who would take responsibility for recovery, not just bask in success.

The other team gave him that.

We didn't.

Lesson #1: Risks Don't Kill Deals—Ignoring Them Does

The CFO's question wasn't just tactical. It was emotional. What he was really asking was:

"Will you take the fall with me if this goes wrong?"

We failed to show we would.

Executives don't need perfection. They need protection. They need to know that if the plan breaks down, they won't be the only ones answering for it.

What lost this deal wasn't a bad answer, but the absence of one.

The Room Goes Quiet

Lesson #2: Confidence Isn't About Proof—It's About Ownership

Mike and Lisa brought reference architectures, performance metrics, and industry benchmarks. They brought proof.

But the other team brought presence. They didn't just know the customer's world. They stepped into it and answered the hardest question in the room without flinching.

And that made all the difference.

In high-stakes service sales, deals aren't lost because of gaps in capability. They're lost when you hesitate in moments that demand certainty.

You don't win trust with polish. You win it with courage.

William Anderson

Chapter 2: Integrity in Sales – The Foundation of Lasting Success

People often say that buyers choose those they know, like, and trust. But in service sales, that isn't enough.

They choose the ones they believe won't disappear when things get hard.

It's easy to mistake sales for persuasion (the craft of convincing someone to do what they weren't planning to do). That definition might apply when you're selling a product or pushing a limited-time offer. But when you're selling services, persuasion fades. The real currency becomes trust, not momentary, transactional trust, but sustained, earned trust.

And trust begins with integrity.

Not just integrity on paper. Not just in contracts or compliance policies. But the kind that shows up in every conversation, every decision, especially when the simple answer is to say nothing at all.

It shows up when the delivery team misses a milestone and you're the one making the call. When the proposal lands above expectations. When internal disagreement surfaces after a customer commitment has already been made. When an urgent customer demand crosses into the realm of the unrealistic.

When your number is on the line, tempting you to shave off just enough of the risk to sound more agreeable.

These moments don't announce themselves as tests of integrity. But they are.

And each one leaves a mark on the customer, on your team, and on your reputation.

The Room Goes Quiet

Sales Is the Transfer of Belief

Every seasoned seller knows the feeling. The moment the room changes. When a buyer leans forward, not because of a well-designed slide, not because of a discount, but because they believe you.

They don't need every answer. But they need to believe that *you* believe.

That's what integrity looks like in practice.

When a seller believes in the solution they represent, deeply and without hesitation, it shows. If they don't, it seeps through: in their tone, in their timing, and in the words they choose not to say.

Conviction travels. But so does doubt.

And in high-stakes service deals, where outcomes are uncertain and stakes are personal, doubt is a deal killer. It's not always visible, but it lingers. It slows the deal, erodes confidence, and eventually closes doors.

You Can't Signal Confidence If You Don't Mean It

At some point, every deal reaches the moment where the price is presented. That number isn't just a figure on a slide. It's a mirror.

Buyers don't just evaluate the price. They evaluate *you*.

They watch your delivery. Your posture. Your pace. How you handle the silence that follows.

Do you rush through it? Immediately soften with a qualifier? Offer to "work with them" before they push back?

Those reactions say more than you realize. They suggest uncertainty, a lack of conviction, and a quiet message that maybe even *you* don't believe the price holds, connecting the outcome to real outcomes, real risks, and real results.

And that creates a ripple effect.

It's not a pricing issue. It's a trust issue.

Confidence at the table doesn't come from charisma. It comes from alignment.

When you understand what the service *actually* delivers, and when you believe that the number represents fair value for the transformation it enables, you don't need to overexplain. You don't flinch. You present it clearly and then stay quiet.

Not because you're stubborn. But because you're honest.

And when the price feels off to *you*, it's not the time to tweak your pitch. That's the time to go back and reconnect the dots. Understand what the service actually solves and why it matters. That's where real sales confidence is built.

Buyers don't just push back on numbers. They push back on *people*.

When your confidence in the value is shaky, it affects more than pricing. It affects perception.

You become easier to challenge. Easier to dismiss. In other words, if you can't sell the value, buyers will discount you. And once a buyer starts discounting *you*, the deal rarely recovers.

Curiosity Is the Engine of Integrity

Integrity isn't just about telling the truth. It's about *knowing* what truth to tell.

The Room Goes Quiet

That's why curiosity is non-negotiable.

You can't act in a customer's best interest if you don't understand their context. And you won't understand that context unless you ask better questions, the kind that go beyond scope and timeline.

Curiosity separates the order taker from the trusted advisor.

Most sellers say they listen. What they actually do is wait for an opening. They're not probing or listening for subtext. They're not unpacking the pressures behind the project or mapping the real decision dynamics inside the organization.

Curious sellers ask:

- Why now?
- What changed to make this a priority?
- Who's betting on this? Who's quietly hoping it fails?
- What's already been tried? Why didn't it work?

And then they do something rare. They *listen*.

Because behind every formal request is an informal pressure. A motivation. A fear. A promotion path. The more curious you are, the more of that you'll uncover. And the more you uncover, the more precise your offer becomes.

That's integrity, too.

Precision isn't about throwing features at a problem. It's about solving *the* problem that really matters. The one they might not have put in the RFP.

William Anderson

Your Customer Success Scorecard

The real measure of a salesperson isn't found in the contract signature. It's revealed in what happens next.

The deal is done, and handshakes were exchanged. But then the lights come up, and the delivery team steps in. What they find tells the true story.

Are they met with clarity or confusion?

Do they see alignment or a trail of overpromises?

Does the customer engage with confidence or hesitate, already second-guessing the commitment?

Is the scope solid or immediately under fire?

These signals point back to how the deal was sold.

If each new engagement begins with friction, it's not a project management issue. It's a trust fracture that started earlier in the sales process, in what was said and left unsaid.

You might be closing deals. But if those deals consistently turn into tension, then you're not setting the business up to win. You're handing off a burden disguised as progress.

That isn't success. It's erosion masked as momentum.

Integrity isn't just about what gets signed, but what stands up under pressure. And the moment after the handoff is when integrity is either confirmed or exposed.

The Room Goes Quiet

So ask yourself:

- Are delivery teams relieved when they see your name on the account, or bracing themselves?
- Is the customer more confident after kickoff or less?
- Are you building trust that grows through execution, or evaporates on contact?

That's your audit. Not a dashboard. Not a quota report. A reputation check.

Winning the wrong way will always catch up with you. And in services, there are no clean escapes. What you sell becomes what others must deliver. That chain is only as strong as the truth you put into it.

If you want to sell with impact and stay in the game long enough to matter, then your success scorecard starts after the signature. Not before it.

The Compounding Effect of Integrity

The highest-performing sellers don't just win business. They build belief inside and outside the company. Delivery leads ask to work on their accounts. Product teams seek their feedback. Sales leaders trust their pipelines.

Why? Because they don't game the system. They raise risks early and don't hide behind ambiguity. They tell the truth even when it costs them a win today.

That kind of integrity earns reputation. But it also earns operational advantage.

Over time, it becomes your differentiator. Customers come back, not because you were perfect, but because you were *real*. They bring more business. Bigger business. And they introduce you to peers who need someone they can trust.

Start Here, or Don't Start at All

Integrity in service sales isn't a virtue to aspire to but the cost of entry.

You see it when someone presents pricing without flinching. When they raise concerns, instead of hiding them. When they dig deeper, instead of jumping to solution mode.

It defines who the customer believes you are before the first contract is ever signed. And when that foundation is built, it unlocks the next level: trust.

Trust isn't given. It's earned. And once earned, it scales your access, your influence, and your outcomes.

That's where we're headed next.

In the following chapter, we'll explore how top sellers transition from surface-level conversations to strategic partnerships. How they step into the customer's world, shoulder real accountability, and bring insight that expands beyond the statement of work.

But none of that matters if you skip this first principle.

Integrity is the foundation. Trust is the multiplier.

Chapter 3: The Psychology of B2B Buying – Navigating Fear, Confidence, and Risk in Sales

Everyone wants to believe that B2B decisions are rational.

We talk about due diligence, ROI calculations, approval gates, and project charters as if the entire process is a machine.

But anyone who has been inside a real enterprise sales process knows what really happens behind the scenes: B2B buying is emotional, especially when the stakes are high.

Fear Is the Biggest Deal-Killer of All

A CIO sat across from me, arms crossed, skeptical but quiet. He had heard the proposal. He understood the benefits. But something else was missing.

He wasn't calculating ROI. He was thinking, "If this goes wrong, who takes the fall?"

That's the real math. And in complex service sales, it often outweighs the financial model.

Remember the multi-million-dollar deal from chapter 1? The buyer killed it because he didn't trust the consultant to protect his political capital. It wasn't the solution, the technical scope, the architecture, or even a soft business case. He just didn't feel safe. No one said it out loud. The official response was "lack of alignment," but the real reason was fear.

And in service sales, fear is the biggest deal-killer in the room.

It doesn't show up in redline edits. It shows up in delayed responses, noncommittal feedback, and that vague discomfort no one puts in writing.

Confidence opens doors. But fear quietly shuts them without confrontation or explanation.

If you don't know how to recognize and neutralize that fear, you will lose deals without ever knowing why.

Why Buying Feels Risky

Behind every complex services purchase is an executive team asking one question: "What happens if this goes badly?"

When an executive signs off on a project, they're putting more than budget at risk. They're putting their credibility, political capital, team focus, and personal bandwidth on the line. If the project misses, they take the hit. They lose influence, leverage, and sometimes, they lose their jobs.

When you're selling services, you're not just competing on capability. You're competing on *how much risk* the buyer feels when working with you.

And the higher the risk, the more likely they are to delay, avoid, or retreat, regardless of how good your proposal is.

Red Flags That You're Not the Safe Choice

You'll know the buyer is still uncertain if they:

- Ask for "one more meeting" before making a decision
- Bring in more voices late in the cycle
- Go quiet after weeks of momentum
- Ask increasingly narrow questions to "get comfortable"
- Hyperfocus on contractual language instead of outcomes
- Ask what happens if things go off track, and they don't like the answer

The Room Goes Quiet

These are not signs of healthy diligence but of emotional hesitation.

Your champion might still want you to win. But someone in the room doesn't feel protected.

How to De-Risk the Decision

There's only one reliable way to overcome fear in a deal. Give the buyer a plan for what happens if things go wrong.

That doesn't mean you assume failure. It means you build confidence by showing how you'll *respond to uncertainty*, not just execute the plan.

Every high-trust sales conversation should include:

- An escalation path with named roles
- An example of how you've recovered from setbacks in similar accounts
- Language that shows shared accountability (e.g., "we'll carry that weight with you")
- Early warning systems, check-ins, and recovery gates
- Clarity on how the project will avoid drift, distraction, and misalignment
- A direct conversation about what "failure" looks like and how you'll prevent it

This makes you the lowest-risk option in the room, even if your price is higher.

Because the buyer doesn't just want results. They want predictability.

Situation: The Technical Win That Never Closed

A mid-sized software company had evaluated three partners for a critical modernization effort. Our team led across every metric, technical capability, industry experience, price, and even relationship depth.

We had the CIO's support. The project had executive sponsorship. We were asked to prepare a kickoff plan.

Then the CFO got involved. He asked one question during the final call:

"If we get halfway through and our timelines shift, what happens?"

Our team responded with process language. They shared how projects are reviewed and how realignment happens. But they didn't answer the underlying question.

"If I back this deal and it slips, do I get hung out to dry?"

No one said no. Instead, there was silence that left the risk unaddressed. And in that silence, the fear was left to linger.

The deal was paused, then postponed, and finally, deprioritized.

Six months later, it was awarded to a vendor who had never led a single technical round. But they had one thing: a mitigation plan.

They showed what would happen if the CFO's timeline moved.

They named names and included executive-level governance.

They shared examples from similar environments and showed they understood what was really at stake.

They didn't win on paper. They won because they made the decision feel safer.

The Room Goes Quiet

Selling to the Real Decision-Maker: Emotion

No one likes to admit they're afraid. Especially not executives.

That's why B2B buying often looks rational but plays out emotionally.

Your champion may believe in the vision. The team may love your solution. But if someone in the decision chain is quietly unsure, the deal stalls or dies without ever naming fear as the reason.

The job of the service seller is to navigate that landscape, give the customer a plan they can trust, and carry uncertainty *with* them, not just pitch around it.

To make the decision safer than standing still. Because until you've sold past fear, you haven't closed anything.

Where We Go From Here

Selling services isn't about closing paperwork. It's about creating enough trust that a buyer is willing to bet their name on you.

In this chapter, we've unpacked the real forces behind that trust: fear, confidence, and emotional risk. But buyers aren't the only ones navigating internal politics and invisible hesitation.

In the next chapter, we'll explore how to navigate the emotional landscape of stakeholders, from your internal champion to the skeptical CFO, and build trust across the full decision-making chain.

Services aren't bought by personas. They're bought by people. And every person has something they're trying to protect.

William Anderson

Case Study: Trust Wins Deals

The Setup: Overcoming Deep Skepticism

This deal wasn't about beating another consulting firm. It was about overcoming skepticism.

The director I met with, Kathleen, had seen it all before: consulting firms with polished presentations, big promises, and vague execution plans. They all claimed to have the perfect strategy. And yet, time after time, they walked away with their fees while her team was left struggling to implement half-baked recommendations.

Kathleen wasn't just skeptical. She was tired of being sold a dream that never materialized. The real challenge wasn't proving we were the best. It was getting her to believe this time would be different.

Breaking Through: Trust Over Theory

Walking into the meeting, I could feel the tension. Kathleen had agreed to the conversation, but she wasn't invested. Her posture was closed, and her questions were clipped. This wasn't a buyer eager to explore options, but someone waiting to be disappointed.

I put my slides away.
 "How many times have you been handed a strategy that never made it past the PowerPoint stage?"

She exhaled, shaking her head. "Too many."

"Yeah, we hear that a lot." I leaned in. "Let's not do that. Tell me, what's the one thing that absolutely has to happen in the next ninety days?"

The Room Goes Quiet

That changed everything.

Her shoulders relaxed just a little. She paused, then said, "We're supposed to have an implementation done by next quarter, but it's completely stalled. My team is stretched thin, leadership is expecting results, and every week that goes by, I lose credibility."

There it was.

This wasn't just about a stalled project. This was personal. This was about Kathleen's reputation, her standing within the company, and her ability to lead under pressure. That was the real problem we needed to solve.

The Emotional Side of Buying: Reading the Signals

Deals are never just about cost, scope, or capabilities. They're about emotion, risk, and belief. If you're paying attention, buyers will tell you what they actually need, not just in words, but in what they emphasize, what frustrates them, and what they fear.

I knew we had to shift the conversation. Kathleen:

- asked about execution, not our expertise. That meant she didn't need another advisor but rather a team that would get their hands dirty.
- mentioned her credibility. That meant this was bigger than just a deliverable; she needed to see progress fast, something she could put in front of leadership.
- talked about the pressure she was under. That meant she wasn't just buying service but looking for someone she could trust to make her look good.

Trust Is Built in the Room

Instead of pitching our capabilities, I proved we understood her reality.

"Look, we both know strategy doesn't mean much if no one can execute it. Let's get specific. Here's what we're going to do in the first two weeks. The first five conversations we'll have. The first blockers we'll clear. And the first updates you'll be able to give your leadership."

Kathleen sat forward. "You're not talking about a framework."

I nodded. "Because no one gets promoted for frameworks. They get promoted for results."

For the first time in the meeting, she smiled. "That's the first thing I've heard today that actually makes sense."

The Moment the Deal Was Won

Even with that shift, one last hesitation came in the final meeting.

"I need to know you won't just tell me what I already know."

I didn't hesitate. "If you already know it, we'll skip it. You don't need a consultant to tell you what's wrong. You need someone to help fix it. That's why we're here."

She took a breath, let it out, and nodded. "Alright. Let's do this."

The Outcome: Trust Turned into Action

We embedded inside Kathleen's team immediately, not as outsiders, but as execution partners. Within the first two weeks, the project was moving again. She had updates to put in front of leadership, and the pressure started to ease.

What started as a single engagement expanded into a long-term partnership. Kathleen didn't just get a consultant, but a team she trusted to make her successful.

The Room Goes Quiet

Key Takeaways: Why Trust Wins

- People don't buy consulting services. They buy belief. They need to believe you'll deliver when it matters.
- Trust isn't built in a proposal. It's built into the conversation. Buyers don't care how much you know until they trust you to execute.
- Emotions drive decisions more than logic. If you don't address the real fears, risks, credibility, and internal politics, you're not actually selling.
- Execution builds long-term partnerships. When clients see immediate impact, you stop being a vendor and start being indispensable.

Trust wins the deal, and execution keeps it. Kathleen didn't need another roadmap. She needed proof that someone would stand with her when it mattered. We gave her that. And in the end, she won internally because we delivered externally.

Chapter 4: The Strategic Partnership Framework – Moving Beyond Traditional Service Sales

Service sales have changed. The rules most organizations still follow (credential-driven messaging, methodology-first positioning, and personality-based relationship selling) are no longer reliable levers. Buyers remain engaged but commit less. Projects get socialized but not prioritized. Consensus is hard to find, and urgency even harder.

This shift isn't subtle. It's structural.

What's required now is not more polish but a repositioning of how sellers show up. Not just what they offer, but how they build trust, create momentum, and navigate complexity.

The Four Pillars of Strategic Partnership framework is designed for that purpose. It offers a clear and repeatable model for elevating the seller's position from transactional vendor to strategic execution partner, consistently, credibly, and under pressure.

The Four Pillars of Strategic Partnership

At the heart of every high-value, high-trust service engagement are four interdependent disciplines. When these are present, deals move faster, scope expands, and influence grows. When they're absent, progress stalls.

- Pillar 1 – Strategic Trust Building: Trust extends beyond credibility. It is built when sellers demonstrate risk ownership, align with internal dynamics, and present with clarity in high-stakes environments.
- Pillar 2 – Value Translation: Effective sellers do not

The Room Goes Quiet

rely on feature-function alignment. They translate technical capabilities into business impact, framed in terms of revenue protection, operational stability, and executive defensibility.
- Pillar 3 – Multilevel Influence: Most enterprise decisions involve competing priorities. Influence is established by harmonizing those perspectives into a shared vision of success, navigable across functional and political lines.
- Pillar 4 – Risk-Based Momentum: The cost of inaction must be made visible. Sellers create urgency by quantifying what delay, or misalignment, means in financial, operational, or reputational terms, turning uncertainty into a reason to act.

Each of these four pillars supports and reinforces the others. When one is weak, the entire pursuit becomes more vulnerable.

Common Failure Patterns

In practice, failed opportunities rarely collapse due to price, proposal structure, or technical fit. More often, they fail quietly because of an absence in one of the four areas above.

The buyer may have trusted the firm's expertise, but doubted its resolve to carry accountability when things became difficult.

The solution may have been sound, but it lacked language that resonated at the business or executive level. The champion may have been strong, but internal resistance was never neutralized. Or the case for change was credible, but it was not compelling.

These breakdowns are avoidable. The framework exists not only to describe these dynamics but also to correct them in-flight.

For sellers actively engaged in pursuit, applying this lens retroactively to a stalled or stagnant opportunity often reveals which strategic muscle needs to be reactivated.

Audience-Specific Application

While the Four Pillars apply universally, their interpretation varies by stakeholder. The most effective sellers understand how to calibrate their posture and message accordingly:

- With technical and operational leaders, trust is earned through subject matter fluency and pragmatic realism. Value is framed in terms of stability, speed, and system performance.
- With mid-level sponsors, trust is built through transparency and alignment to visible, promotable outcomes. Value becomes the ability to deliver against internal expectations.
- With executive decision-makers, trust is less about scope execution and more about reputational safety. They look for clarity, control, and the assurance that risk will be owned. Value is measured in what they can confidently defend.

As stakeholder altitude increases, the emotional weight of the decision often increases alongside it. The ability to demonstrate risk absorption and narrative clarity becomes more important than technical excellence.

A Practical Illustration

Consider a services team positioning an automation framework for a global manufacturer:

- Trust is built when they identify a security exposure the internal team had not previously flagged and demonstrate a plan to resolve it without escalation
- Value is translated not as improved workflows, but as a documented $6.2 million in recovered throughput based on reduced downtime
- Influence is orchestrated across the CIO, operations leadership, and finance, each of whom enters the conversation with different concerns but exits aligned to a unified three-quarters roadmap for outcomes

The Room Goes Quiet

- Momentum is created by modeling the cost of delay: on-time delivery risk, downstream revenue leakage, and executive sponsor exposure

This is not theoretical differentiation. It is execution-led selling, anchored in relevance and owned risk.

The Strategic Imperative

The market no longer rewards clever positioning or cleverer PowerPoint presentations.

What buyers want is protection. What they need is confidence.

This framework offers a repeatable approach to earning both through posture, structure, and practical alignment. It is designed for teams that need to sell at enterprise scale without losing human fidelity. And it equips them to shift the conversation from services and scope to risk, timing, and value.

In a procurement-led, trust-constrained landscape, that shift is the difference between being evaluated and being invited.

Looking Ahead

This chapter outlined the structure.

The chapters that follow will offer the system: breaking down how each pillar operates across the sales lifecycle, how it adapts to different deal scenarios, and how to recover when one has been neglected.

The next chapter presents a case study in which this framework was used to win a complex engagement, despite internal skepticism and stronger technical competition. It highlights how trust, clarity, and momentum, properly sequenced, can reshape a buying decision.

For practitioners and leaders alike, this framework is not simply a model for understanding the current state. It is a tool for changing it.

William Anderson

Case Study: How Trust, Clarity, and Risk Ownership Won the Deal

The Setup: When Credibility Matters More Than Capability

The RFP had already gone out.

Three vendors were shortlisted. On paper, the project appeared to be routine: modernize the front-desk check-in system across 40 hotels, migrate guest data to the cloud, and tie it all into pricing and inventory logic.

But when the team sat down with Anaya, Senior Manager of Enterprise Systems at the customer, they could tell this wasn't about capability. It was about credibility.

She had survived two major systems overhauls in the past five years. One had strengthened her influence. The other had left scars: budget overruns, delayed go-lives, and trust lost with her executive sponsors.

This initiative was more than a system upgrade.

It was a test of her judgment. And she couldn't afford to get it wrong.

Earning the Conversation, By Naming the Risk
(Pillar 1: Strategic Trust Building)

Anaya opened the meeting in a direct manner.

"We're not doing another proof of concept. I've seen the demos. I need to know what happens when it fails."

The team didn't flinch. They didn't reach for the deck. They didn't quote Service Level Agreements (SLAs).

The Room Goes Quiet

They walked her through five failure modes they'd seen in hospitality rollouts like this:

- Site-specific configuration drift between hotels that destabilizes check-in integrations
- Peak-time outages cause staff to revert to pen and paper, losing system continuity
- Untrained desk agents create local workarounds that corrupt guest data
- Time zone-misaligned updates that trigger shutdowns during local business hours
- Desynchronized loyalty databases between hotel and corporate systems

And they didn't stop there.

They showed how they'd respond, who gets paged, what steps are taken, and what happens in the first forty-eight hours after a failure.

It wasn't risk avoidance. It was risk ownership.

That's when Anaya started listening, not defensively but as someone looking for a partner.

Co-Creation Over Persuasion
(Pillar 2: Value Translation)

Rather than delivering a polished vendor slide deck, the team offered to help build the internal narrative Anaya and her leader would need.

Together, they developed a proposal that reframed the project as brand protection and operational continuity, not just guest check-in automation. They mapped system resilience to real business impact: occupancy conversion rates, loyalty capture accuracy, and revenue predictability during peak load.

It was practical. It was specific. And it sounded like Anaya's voice, not a vendor's.

By the time they presented to the CIO, Anaya and her director weren't relaying someone else's pitch.

They were leading the room.

Alignment Without Friction
(Pillar 3: Multilevel Influence)

The team didn't try to force consensus. They mapped it.

They met with guest experience, finance, and property ops leaders. Each had different concerns, such as desk usability, budget clarity, and rollout timing. But instead of collapsing them into a generic alignment, the team preserved each perspective and wove them together into one delivery roadmap.

When the final proposal was circulated, every stakeholder saw their fingerprints on it.

No one had to be convinced. They already saw their priorities reflected.

Making Waiting Feel Riskier Than Moving
(Pillar 4: Risk-Based Momentum)

Anaya still hesitated.

"This changes how 40 hotels operate. That kind of shift doesn't go unnoticed."

The team didn't push. They modeled the cost of delay.

What would it mean for loyalty program misfires to persist for another twelve months?

The Room Goes Quiet

What would happen if occupancy forecasting continued with stale or partial check-in data?

How would it feel to answer once again why the last modernization didn't fully land?

The data wasn't dramatic. It was clear, and clarity creates urgency.

Anaya didn't need to be sold. She needed to see that moving forward was the safer option.

She saw it and closed the folder.

"Let's get this moving."

What Made the Difference

This deal wasn't won through superior demos. It wasn't won by pushing harder or discounting faster.

It was won through consistent, credible execution of the Four Pillars:

- Strategic Trust Building was earned early by naming where projects fail (not hiding from it) and showing how the team would absorb risk under pressure
- Value Translation reframed check-in automation as a business-critical enabler tied to loyalty, revenue precision, and brand delivery, not a tech refresh
- Multilevel Influence created alignment by amplifying stakeholder needs rather than diluting them, empowering the internal team to lead with confidence
- Risk-Based Momentum was established by modeling delay as a threat to executive perception, not just technical progress and making the safe path the bold one

William Anderson

Anaya didn't say yes because she was persuaded.

She said yes because she saw herself succeeding inside the story they built together.

That's what execution looks like.

And that's what strategic selling demands.

Chapter 5: From Insight to Execution – What Comes Next Isn't Theory

You've already seen the shift. Maybe it was the deal that circled for weeks before disappearing. The champion who went quiet. The exec who nodded but never followed up. The champions who support the deal privately but won't commit publicly. Buying processes that look complete on paper, but stall without warning.

This first section hasn't told you anything you didn't already know in your gut.

What it has done is to name and frame it, and begin to point toward what to do about it.

The rules of service selling have changed. Instinct isn't enough anymore.

You need a model. A system. A way to win without waiting for the perfect buyer or the perfect timing.

That's what the Strategic Partnership Framework offers.

The Shift We Just Made

In the first chapters, we moved from transactional thinking to strategic posture.

We examined what modern buyers actually fear and what they need to believe.

We reframed service selling as an act of trust ownership, not solution pitching.

We introduced the Four Pillars that top performers use to create leverage where others have none:

- Strategic Trust Building as a deliberate act of risk absorption
- Value Translation as a muscle for turning capabilities into business meaning
- Multilevel Influence as a skill in managing political alignment, not just technical agreement
- Risk-Based Momentum as the pressure buyers need to move, not stall

And we've seen those principles at work, both when missed and when mastered.

This wasn't mindset work for its own sake.

It was laying the foundation for how execution must now look.

Where Most Teams Stall

It's not at the pitch. It's after.

After the deck is sent, and the meeting ends with smiles and nods.

After the champion says, "This looks great. I'll share it internally."

That's where most teams lose control.

Not because their solution was wrong. Not because the customer didn't like them. But because they didn't own what came next.

They assumed trust had been earned when it was still conditional. They believed the value was understood when it hadn't been translated. They accepted progress as a signal of momentum when it was only motion. They handed the pen to the buyer without checking whether the story was strong enough to carry forward. And when the deal stalled or disappeared, they chalked it up to timing, or budget, or politics.

The real issue wasn't alignment. It was absence. They weren't present in the next conversation because they never equipped the buyer to have it. That's the execution gap.

The Room Goes Quiet

In today's market, that's where deals die quietly, and this is where we'll begin. Bridging that gap is the difference between strong ideas and real outcomes.

What Comes Next

Most teams don't fail because they don't understand the buyer. They fail because they hesitate right at the moment action is required. They get the insight, believe in the framework, and nod in agreement during enablement sessions. And then?

They go back to chasing deals with the same old habits. They keep overpreparing decks instead of preparing the room. They lead with "what we do" instead of "what's at risk." They try to prove value instead of helping the buyer feel protected.

And when the deal slows, they wait. They re-engage. They resend the proposal. They don't recover. They don't shift. They stall—because they haven't built the muscle for what to do next.

This next section is where that changes. We're done talking about why the game is different.

Now we'll talk about how to win.

You'll learn how to walk into a first meeting and establish strategic trust without a single slide. How to spot the hidden fear behind a budget delay and pull it into the open. How to turn quiet stakeholders into active champions without putting your champion at risk. And how to name risk in a room full of executives and earn more credibility, not less.

Because the difference between average and exceptional isn't who has better messaging. It's who knows what to do when momentum falters, the room goes quiet, or politics surface mid-deal.

The next chapters are about that. Not theory. Not hope, but execution.

Turn the page. Let's move.

Part II: Building Trust Through Strategic Alignment

The Room Goes Quiet

Chapter 6: Who Really Sells the Work?

Selling services is rarely straightforward. It doesn't fit neatly into a traditional sales organisation chart, and it rarely belongs to a single title. In professional services, selling is a team sport, but one where the rules, players, and scoreboard shift depending on the company, the client, and the moment.

What makes services sales unique isn't just that you're selling effort instead of a product. It's that you're asking the customer to believe in you as a path to their own success. You're selling credibility, not code. You're selling certainty, not software. You're selling the belief that your team can walk into ambiguity and still deliver.

To do that, you need more than a closer, more than a relationship. You need a set of roles, each with a different angle on value, risk, and execution that collectively earn trust, manage delivery, and drive the deal forward.

But these roles aren't always defined. In most organizations, especially in services-led businesses, they're shaped more by behavior than by title. And in the field, who actually "sells the work" often depends less on who owns the number and more on who holds the room when things get uncertain.

This next set of chapters breaks that down.

We start with the five dominant archetypes that appear again and again in successful services organizations, not as official job descriptions, but as recognizable patterns. Then we explore how those roles function differently depending on the company type: whether you're inside a software giant trying to grow services around a product, a consulting firm trying to land new engagements through relationships, or a systems integrator bidding against six competitors for a multimillion-dollar implementation.

William Anderson

Each archetype has strengths, blind spots, and unique interfaces with both sales and delivery. And each business model creates a different set of constraints, incentives, and expectations for how service sales actually happens.

If you're a seller, this will help you recognize where you thrive and where you may need a partner. If you're a leader, this will give you a map of how to structure, align, and equip your team based on your company's DNA. And if you're trying to win more often, this will show you why most failed deals never fell apart in front of the customer. They fell apart internally when the wrong people carried the wrong parts of the conversation.

Understanding who really sells the work in your world isn't just helpful. It's foundational.

Chapter 7: The Service Seller Archetypes

Services aren't sold by one person. They're sold through a constellation of roles, each carrying a piece of the credibility and each filling in part of the risk picture. But in most organizations, those roles aren't clearly defined. They emerge in practice, shaped by habit, organizational structure, or necessity.

After watching hundreds of deals succeed and fail, it is clear that there are five distinct archetypes that appear again and again across service-led organizations. They may have different titles, compensation plans, or levels of authority, but their behavior is unmistakable.

These aren't hypothetical constructs. These are the roles that show up when real work is on the line.

Understanding these archetypes and the gaps between them is critical. Most breakdowns in service sales don't happen because of pricing, competition, or customer pushback. They happen internally when the people responsible for carrying the sale aren't aligned, or worse, aren't aware of who's really doing the selling.

The Closer

Of the five archetypes, the Closer embodies the most traditional sales persona. They're often quota-carrying, pipeline-focused, and trained in standard enterprise selling methodology. They understand how to work the account, read the buying signals, and navigate procurement. The Closer is at their best in deal rooms, forecasting calls, and negotiating contracts.

Their power is urgency. They know how to move an opportunity forward, ask for the close, and hold firm under pressure. In services, this can be a differentiator, especially when the other voices in the deal are more delivery-focused and hesitant to challenge the client.

But the Closer has blind spots. They often lack a deep understanding of delivery nuances or technical feasibility. They may overpromise regarding the scope, underrepresent risk, or treat the services sale like a product sale, assuming that certainty can be manufactured rather than earned.

Where they succeed: In organizations where services are packaged and repeatable, and where pricing and negotiation are complex and customer-facing

Where they struggle: In bespoke consulting environments where credibility must be built on executional fluency and problem-solving depth.

Key interfaces: Pre-sales architects, pricing teams, regional delivery leads, legal, and commercial operations

When paired well with an Architect or Consultant-as-Seller, the Closer can drive velocity without compromising trust. When they are left solo, they risk selling something no one else can deliver.

The Architect

The Architect is the one the customer trusts to tell the truth.

They are technical, functional, or domain experts who translate business needs into feasible solutions. They know how the work will get done, how long it will take, and where the risks are buried. Often, they're brought into the sales cycle to validate the approach, scope the effort, or design the solution itself.

Their power is credibility. Customers instinctively believe the Architect over the Closer. They ask smarter questions, acknowledge complexity, and build confidence through thoughtful precision. When an Architect says, "We can do that," it holds more weight than any proposal language or marketing deck.

But Architects often avoid commercial conversations. Many have been burned by sellers overpromising on scope or

The Room Goes Quiet

discounting without understanding effort. As a result, they may lean toward caution or unintentionally stall momentum. They can also overbuild solutions, solving for every edge case instead of anchoring to what the customer actually needs to move forward.

Where they succeed: In complex, high-risk deals where execution confidence is the deciding factor

Where they struggle: In fast-moving sales environments where speed, pricing flexibility, and storytelling matter as much as accuracy

Key interfaces: Delivery teams, solution architects, pursuit teams, and client technical stakeholders

The best Architects are embedded in early sales motion, not just pulled in to approve scope. They bring value not only in accuracy, but in making the customer feel like the team truly understands their world.

The Consultant-as-Seller

Some of the best services salespeople don't carry a number. They carry a relationship.

The Consultant-as-Seller is embedded in delivery. They've earned the customer's trust not through promises, but through presence. They've been in the room when things went sideways and helped pull the team through it. They know the politics inside the customer's org, who has influence, and who's just making noise.

Their power is proximity. They see unmet needs before they're formally voiced. They know when a pilot is about to expand, when an executive is looking for a champion, or when a new budget line is being opened quietly. They surface opportunities not through outbound activity, but through situational awareness and earned trust.

But most Consultants-as-Sellers are uncomfortable with pricing, negotiation, or deal strategy. They often rely on others to formalize the scope and write the proposal. That's fine until the pursuit loses momentum or commercial alignment breaks down.

Where they succeed: In post-sale expansion, relationship-driven accounts, and consultative growth

Where they struggle: In net-new pursuits, competitive RFPs, and pricing-sensitive negotiations

Key interfaces: Delivery leadership, customer sponsors, practice leaders, and engagement managers

This archetype is one of the most powerful engines of growth in professional services. *If* they're supported by commercial partners who can operationalize and capture the value they identify.

The Service Manager

The Service Manager isn't always seen as part of the sales motion, but they should be.

They own the day-to-day experience of the customer. They run QBRs, manage escalations, and keep delivery aligned to contractual obligations. In many organizations, they are the most visible and consistent point of contact once the work begins.

Their power is accountability. They speak with authority because they're responsible for outcomes. When they say a team will deliver, customers believe it. When they escalate an issue, customers pay attention. When they suggest a next step, it's often acted on without needing a full pursuit motion.

But Service Managers are often stretched thin. They carry too many accounts, get pulled into firefighting, and rarely have the time or mandate to develop strategic conversations. And

The Room Goes Quiet

because they're measured on operational success, they may avoid introducing risk, even when opportunity is present.

Where they succeed: In renewal cycles, managed service relationships, and accounts where continuity is key.

Where they struggle: In proactive growth, white-space opportunity identification, and transformational change

Key interfaces: Delivery directors, account teams, customer operations, and support escalation teams

When paired with a Strategist or Consultant-as-Seller, the Service Manager becomes a force multiplier. They see the signals first. They just need the space and support to act on them.

The Strategist

The Strategist sees the long game.

They operate at the account level, sometimes across multiple accounts, guiding positioning, identifying growth themes, and connecting service offerings to the customer's broader business objectives. They are often aligned to verticals, transformation agendas, or innovation initiatives.

Their power is alignment. They speak the customer's language, think in outcomes, and operate with executive altitude. They frame consulting and services not as labor or support, but as instruments of change. When positioned well, they open doors no one else can.

But Strategists can drift too far from execution. Their visions aren't always grounded in delivery capability or timeline realism. Without strong ties with practitioners and delivery leads, they risk overpromising or creating disconnects between expectation and capacity.

Where they succeed: In long-cycle growth, executive engagement, and multiyear roadmaps

Where they struggle: In transactional pursuits, hands-on scoping, and rapid response cycles

Key Interfaces: Client executives, industry leads, solution marketing, and consulting leadership

When Strategists stay close to the field and regularly recalibrate with the team doing the work, they become catalysts for sustainable growth.

None of these roles sells the deal alone. But together, they form the muscle memory of a high-performing services sales organization.

Success depends not just on having the right roles but on knowing who owns which part of the trust equation at each stage of the deal. Misalignment here doesn't just slow things down. It erodes credibility, breaks momentum, and loses winnable opportunities.

If you don't know which archetypes are showing up in your pursuits, or worse, if the customer sees a gap in the room, it's only a matter of time before the deal goes quiet.

Chapter 8: Modern Models – When Services Are the Reason Deals Succeed

Services are no longer confined to traditional consulting firms or systems integrators. Today, they're embedded, sometimes visibly and sometimes reluctantly, into nearly every business model that sells complexity, scale, or strategic outcomes.

The companies that win with services aren't just selling time, scope, or effort. They're selling executional confidence. The difference is that in some businesses, confidence is an afterthought. In others, it's the only thing that keeps the customer relationship from falling apart.

This chapter walks through how services sales roles show up and often compete for ownership within today's most common business models. From cloud-native hyperscalers to hybrid platform-consulting companies to boutique agencies, the dynamics may change, but the stakes remain the same. If no one owns the work, the customer won't trust the outcome.

SaaS Platforms (Product-Led Growth, Enterprise B2B)

In product-led SaaS companies, services are typically positioned as onboarding, enablement, or support, not value creation. The business assumes simplicity, but enterprise customers often need deeper support, integration, and strategy.

Sales ownership is fractured. Account executives (AEs) sell licenses. Customer Success owns retention. Architects scope solutions. Consultant-as-Seller and Service Manager roles are missing or underpowered.

This creates a trust gap. When implementations stall or results lag, services become the backstop, but no one is accountable for making them succeed.

Mature SaaS firms build bridge roles between CS, sales, and delivery. They treat services not as a reactive fix, but as a proactive multiplier of retention and renewal.

Cloud Providers (AWS, Google Cloud, Azure, Alibaba)

Cloud providers don't "sell" services in the traditional sense, but services are the lever that drives consumption. Internal solution architects, TAMs, and field CS teams deliver architectural guidance and enablement workshops that, while not commercialized, shape usage.

These roles are *execution-centric but commercially passive*. The Strategist and Architect archetypes are strong, but the Closer is often missing. Services revenue isn't tracked or owned.

The result is that services are critical to value realization, but no one owns the risk. Trust is built in the field but not reinforced by commercial accountability.

Cloud providers that win in the long term use partner-delivered services to fill the gap and build internal overlays that understand both platform architecture and customer transformation goals.

AI/ML and Data-Native Companies

These businesses are product-driven in brand, but service-dependent in practice. Customers don't know how to implement AI. They don't trust the output and often lack the talent to apply insights.

Execution is the product, but the services motion is often hidden under the guise of enablement or "customer activation."

Closers push product, while Architects do all the heavy lifting. Consultants-as-Sellers and Strategists, by contrast, are often underfunded or operate informally.

Winning in this model requires recognizing that services are not a supplement, but the differentiator. Success comes from embedding delivery partners, training architects to sell value,

The Room Goes Quiet

and supporting trusted execution with commercial structure.

Platform and Consulting Hybrids (Salesforce, ServiceNow, Oracle, Adobe)

These companies walk a fine line. They are product-first companies, often with embedded consulting teams, and serve enterprise customers with both licenses and strategic support.

Internal friction is constant. Sales wants to control the relationship. Partners want protection. Internal consulting wants to expand. No one is quite sure who owns what.

The Strategist shows up late or is politically sidelined. The Consultant-as-Seller earns trust inside delivery, but rarely carries weight in the roadmap or commercial decisions. Closers chase licenses, not long-term value.

The best of these companies create rules of engagement for services. They define when to lead, when to support, and how internal teams complement rather than compete with partner ecosystems.

Digital Agencies and Creative-Technical Firms

These firms sell transformation through experience, design, or innovation. They lead with vision, deliver with speed, and often straddle the line between strategic advisor and build partner.

The Consultant-as-Seller and Architect archetypes dominate. Strategists guide positioning. Closers exist but often step aside once the client is emotionally committed. The sale happens through trust in vision and fluency in execution.

These firms excel in **narrative-led sales tied to visible outcomes.** They struggle with pricing discipline, timeline control, and managing delivery risk in an evolving scope.

Growth requires grounding creative selling with operational structure, ensuring the pitch isn't just inspirational, but executable.

Software Companies (Traditional Enterprise ISVs)

Traditional software vendors often treat services as **post-sale problem solvers**. They're included to accelerate adoption or reduce churn, not to lead transformation.

AEs are product-focused and rarely incentivized to push services. Pre-sales architects try to scope effort, but the follow-through is usually lacking. The Consultant-as-Seller and Service Manager roles are underdeveloped.

The result is scope mismatch, strained delivery, and underleveraged growth potential. Customers buy licenses and get vague promises. Services becomes the team that *fixes* what was missed in pre-sales.

Modernizing this model means **reframing services as the outcome assurance layer.** Strategists need air cover. Consultants-as-Sellers need formalized responsibility. And delivery voices need presence *before* the deal closes.

Value-Added Resellers (VARs)

In the VAR world, services are tied to the product attach rate. They're scoped to fulfill, not to transform. Most services are standardized: install, configure, support.

The Closer drives the conversation. The Architect validates scope. The Service Manager owns outcomes but only post-sale. Strategists and Consultants-as-Sellers are rare, if they exist at all.

When the deal is simple, this works. When the account grows in complexity, the lack of strategic services posture becomes a risk.

Mature VARs expand by **investing in consultative overlays**, building vertical practices, and shifting from transactional

The Room Goes Quiet

services to outcome-based engagements.

Managed Services Providers (MSPs)

MSPs are defined by SLAs, continuity, and operational discipline. Services are the product, but the value is measured in uptime, not strategy.

Closers manage renewals and pricing. Service Managers carry the customer relationship. Consultant-as-Seller roles surface growth in existing contracts but are often reactive. Architects provide design expertise in expansion or remediation.

The sales motion is tied tightly to risk mitigation. The downside is that few of these firms build Strategist roles to shape longer-term transformation narratives. Customers see stability but not innovation.

Leaders in this space evolve by **investing in customer strategy functions** that help clients not just stabilize but modernize.

Pure-Play Consulting Firms

In pure-play consultancies, everyone sells. But few carry quotas.

The Consultant-as-Seller is the dominant archetype. Engagement leads build trust and expand organically. Architects provide scoping. Strategists engage at the executive level to shape roadmaps. Closers are often invisible or only activated in pursuit structuring.

The strength here is credibility. The weakness is commercial inconsistency. Deals vary in quality, process, and defensibility. Pursuits are often relationship-led but unsupported by formal enablement.

Firms that scale solve this with **intentional pursuit strategies**, partner-led overlays, and structured scoping teams. They protect trust while maturing sales hygiene.

System Integrators

Integrators are execution machines. Their services are large-scale, high-risk, and multiyear.

Sales motions here are orchestral. Closers manage pricing and pursuit governance. Architects build scope and resource plans. Service Managers manage post-sale outcomes. Consultants-as-Sellers may lead embedded accounts. Strategists position transformational plays across towers.

Where this breaks down is in ownership. Pursuit teams are large, and the roles blur. Customers sense internal noise. Delivery gets misrepresented. The deal stalls.

The best integrators align roles *before* the pursuit starts. They define the voice of the customer, pursuit owner, and escalation pathways. They know who's in the room and why.

Field Insight

There is no universal model. But there is a universal truth: **services are sold through clarity.**

In every business, whether the services are visible, buried, or unofficial, someone is carrying the credibility, and someone is carrying the risk. When that's not clearly owned, deals go quiet. Scope misaligns. Execution wobbles.

The companies that win don't just structure the work. They structure who *owns* the work.

That structure is what sets up everything that follows. Once a deal is won, the promises made by sales must become realities delivered by the field. And if the customer can't see a continuity between those two worlds, trust gets replaced with fear.

That's where we go next.

Chapter 9: Understanding Customer Behavior & Strategic Empathy in Service Sales

A sale is never just a transaction. It is a sequence of human decisions, shaped not by logic alone, but by psychology, pressure, and the unseen weight each stakeholder carries.

We talk about phases: initial interest, internal evaluation, procurement review, executive approval, but the emotional movement begins long before those decision points. It begins with belief.

The most successful sales professionals understand that they're not just navigating processes. They're navigating people.

They recognize that every participant in the buying journey sees the world through a different lens. And they don't just adjust their pitch; they adjust their posture.

They meet customers in their reality and help them see a version of the future that feels not only possible, but necessary.

Typically, the meeting is going exactly as planned, until it isn't. A slide hits too hard. A promise lands wrong. And suddenly, the sponsor who has been leaning in is leaning back.

Empathy isn't about affirming feelings. It's about reading pressure and responding before momentum disappears.

This chapter explores the full depth of that process, from understanding the psychology of each stakeholder to deploying strategic empathy that turns resistance into partnership.

Because in services sales, influence isn't about pressure. It's about presence.

The Psychology of the Champion: The First Believer

Every deal begins with a spark: a champion who sees potential and steps forward. This person doesn't always have the final say, but they have enough conviction to push the conversation forward. And that conviction is fragile.

Their motivation isn't just organizational. They're personal.

Champions are often accountable for solving problems but lack unilateral authority to act. What they're really searching for is credibility. The opportunity to deliver a visible win, to move the needle, and to be seen doing it.

That risk, when aligned with the right partner, becomes fuel. But only if they believe they won't be left exposed.

They need more than a solution. They need backup.

Becoming Their Champion

Champions don't advocate for vendors. They advocate for partners they trust.

That trust is built in the quiet moments: when you help reframe technical detail into executive relevance, when you shape the story in a way that makes your buyer look credible to their peers, and when you offer just enough flexibility in your roadmap that it feels co-created, not imposed.

Strategic sellers don't just influence the champion's thinking. They help the champion shape internal consensus.

The shift is subtle but powerful. It's when your champion says, "Here's what we're working on," instead of, "Here's what they proposed." It's when they ask, "How should I explain this to my CFO?" because they trust you'll make them sound smart, not because they doubt your expertise.

The Room Goes Quiet

That shift is built on four foundational practices.

First, trust isn't earned by pretending nothing will go wrong. It's built by showing exactly how you'll respond when it does.

Second, value must be translated into the buyer's language, not just what your service does, but what it allows them to accomplish or signal inside their organization.

Third, influence isn't about one contact. It's about helping your champion speak credibly across functions and roles.

And fourth, framing risk clearly, not just to push urgency, but to outline the cost of inaction, can do more than any discount or incentive ever could.

When done well, your champion doesn't feel like they're carrying your deal. They feel like you're helping them carry theirs.

The Psychology of Procurement: Guardians of Risk

Once your champion creates momentum, the deal crosses into the domain of procurement.

This is often where progress slows because the lens shifts.

Procurement isn't motivated by transformation. They're incentivized to prevent regret.

Behavioral research shows that people are more sensitive to potential loss than to potential gain, and procurement institutionalizes that fear.

Their job is to protect the organization from unnecessary cost, unclear ROI, and contractual exposure.

To win over procurement, you must shift your language.

Replace vision with verification. Replace possibility with process. Don't ask them to believe. Ask them to approve. And give them what they need to say yes without fear.

The best sellers prepare procurement to defend the decision, not just process it. That means presenting an escalation path with named roles, sharing examples of how they've recovered from setbacks in similar accounts, and using language that signals shared ownership. They use phrases like "We'll carry that weight with you." It also means providing early warning systems and check-ins to prevent misalignment, being clear about how you'll avoid project drift, having direct conversations about what failure could look like, and explaining exactly how you'll prevent it.

The goal isn't to inspire confidence.

It's to eliminate concern.

The Executive Lens: Decisions at the Top

Even with a supportive champion and a cooperative procurement team, final approval often rests with senior executives. Their view is wider.

Executives evaluate deals not just on their standalone merit, but on alignment with strategic imperatives: growth, innovation, resilience, and market momentum.

They trust people over proposals. Relationships matter. So does composure.

Your strongest argument may not be your deck. It's how you carry the room.

At this level, the conversation shifts from cost to consequence. Executives will pay a premium if they believe the investment makes the company better. But they'll walk away from uncertainty.

The Room Goes Quiet

That's why great sellers show executives the broader impact, not just what the service does, but what it makes possible.

Strategic Empathy: Selling the Way Customers Buy

Understanding your customer's world means more than researching their company. It means understanding what's unsaid.

When a CIO discusses cloud migration, they're not listing features. They're broadcasting fear about security, adoption, and timeline credibility.

Strategic empathy is the art of reading the pressure map. Seeing what someone is protecting and why they can't say it out loud.

Understanding Buyer Motivations Across Industries

High performers don't just tailor their messages to personas. They adapt to the operating reality of the customer's industry. That reality defines what risk looks like, what success feels like, and what keeps your buyer up at night.

A great seller doesn't just ask, "What does the customer want?"
They ask, "What are they afraid to lose?"

Let's break it down:

In healthcare, the fear isn't just about money; it's about safety and compliance. A botched implementation or delayed rollout can jeopardize patient outcomes, trigger audits, or compromise regulatory standing. Your buyer might care about efficiency, but what they're really trying to protect is the integrity of care. Speak to that, or you'll sound like someone who doesn't understand the stakes.

In retail, timelines are brutal. A missed go-live doesn't just push back a project, but it could blow an entire promotional season or sink quarterly results. Retail buyers aren't looking for flexibility. They're looking for vendors who won't leave them exposed when calendar pressure turns operational risk into financial pain.

In manufacturing, decisions cascade. What happens in one plant impacts dozens of others. A minor disruption in one region could mean global shipment delays, missed SLAs, or reputational fallout with top-tier clients. The stakes aren't just technical but systemic. That's why manufacturers don't trust theory. They trust precision, uptime, and contingency planning.

In financial services, everything runs through the lens of trust and scrutiny. A flawed rollout isn't just a project failure. It could become a compliance incident, a headline, or an internal credibility loss that follows your champion for years. These buyers assess risk intensely. They don't want promises. They want control, governance, and political cover.

In each industry, fear wears a different face. But it always exists. When you speak directly to the buyer's pressure: what they're defending, what they're trying to prove, and what they can't afford to get wrong, you do more than demonstrate relevance.

You become the only seller they feel safe to say yes to.

Managing the Multistakeholder Landscape

Enterprise decisions are messy. The real skill is not pitching to personas but understanding power and posture.

You need to see:

- Who holds the budget: Identify the person who actually controls the money. This individual can green-light or stop the deal regardless of enthusiasm elsewhere.
- Who can say no when it is too late: Every enterprise has a late-stage veto player such as security, procurement, or a senior executive. If you ignore them, they can sink the deal after months of work.
- Who is on the hook for results: This is the operational leader whose career rises or falls with the project's success. Their buy-in is critical because they will be

The Room Goes Quiet

your internal advocate or your silent saboteur.

- Who is waiting for it to fail: Someone in the organization benefits if the initiative collapses. It might be a rival department, a skeptical executive, or a former vendor trying to return. Anticipating these undercurrents is essential.

Great sellers do not just ask about the org chart. They map influence, hesitation, and trust gaps. They equip champions to build consensus through executive summaries, fallback plans, and decision frameworks that reduce internal risk.

Tactical Empathy: Listening With Presence

Empathy isn't a soft skill. It's a tactical one.

Silence, mirroring, and labeling aren't conversation tricks. They're pressure diffusers.

The best salespeople don't rush to fill space. They allow fear to surface. They stay still enough to read what's really happening.

This is how you sell when fear enters the room:

By standing steady.

What Happens When You Get This Right

When you apply strategic and tactical empathy, the entire sales conversation changes.

You're not selling features. You're offering protection. You're not closing deals. You're guiding movement.

Champions feel backed. Procurement feels safe. Executives see clarity. And you, the seller, no longer look like a vendor.

You look like a person who already belongs in the room.

William Anderson

Case Study: Tactical Empathy in Action

The Setup: Reading the Signals No One Else Saw

The deck was strong, and the demo ran smoothly. The technical story checked every box. But the room felt off.

Rachel, the director of digital programs, a key mid-level stakeholder with outsized influence on the deal, wasn't reacting. She wasn't disengaged, but she also wasn't buying in. No eye contact. No note-taking. No questions. Her expression was neutral. Her arms were crossed. She glanced at the wall clock every few minutes. Occasionally, she'd nod, but always at the wrong moment, like she wasn't tracking content as much as waiting for it to end.

David, the lead architect, pressed on, reviewing API diagrams and projected timelines. He was confident, well-prepared, and stayed on script. On the surface, everything looked fine.

But to Elise, the service seller sitting across from Rachel, the signal from her composed, controlled politeness was clear: this deal was slipping, and no one in the room had noticed.

Elise didn't panic. She paused, watched, and shifted the conversation.

Leading with Presence, Not Pitch

Rather than push the discussion forward, Elise leaned in and mirrored Rachel's earlier language.

"You mentioned earlier that the biggest issue with the last initiative was timing. Speed-to-market is the real pressure here?"

That simple question, mirroring Rachel's own phrasing, stopped the meeting cold. It wasn't a throwaway line. It was intentional. It showed she'd been listening.

The Room Goes Quiet

Rachel looked up. She blinked. And then the shift happened.

"That's exactly it," she said. "We had a rollout that landed two weeks after Black Friday. Everything technically worked, but we missed the window, and I was the one who had to explain it to leadership."

There it was. The emotional anchor behind her detachment.

This wasn't about capability. This was about exposure.

Redirecting the Room with Precision

Elise didn't pivot back to providing solutions. She stayed with it.

"It sounds like you were carrying more of the risk than you expected or were told you would be."

That wasn't a guess. It was a label. A clear, empathetic naming of the unspoken concern in the room.

Rachel paused again and then nodded. "Exactly. The vendor just kept saying 'on track' at every check-in. And then suddenly, we weren't."

Now they were talking. Not about software. About trust.

At that point, David, trying to be helpful, jumped in to offer reassurance: fast-track sprints, tighter QA cycles, and contingency buffers.

But Elise raised her hand slightly, not to silence him, but to redirect. She turned again to Rachel, keeping her voice steady.

"Let's not assume nothing will go wrong. Let's talk about what happens when it does. What kind of visibility do you need, early enough that you're not the one surprised in the executive review?"

That landed.

Rachel leaned in. Her arms uncrossed. She picked up her pen, and for the first time in the meeting, she asked a question.

Why This Seller Won the Deal
The competitors had better slides. Some were cheaper. All had capabilities. But none of them did what Elise did. She:

- Mirrored the buyer's words to show she was listening
- Labeled the real concern without judgment or spin
- Stayed steady when others defaulted to reassurance
- Reframed risk as a shared responsibility, not as a solo burden

She didn't win the deal in that room. But she earned the one thing that leads to winning: the buyer's belief that she would show up when things got hard.

Tactical Empathy Is Execution
This wasn't about charm. It wasn't about EQ theater. This was execution. Elise had done her homework. She knew the timeline failures from the last project weren't technical, but relational. She recognized when the room was stuck and calmly shifted the dynamic.

Empathy wasn't something she used. It was how she worked. She didn't show up to sound confident. She showed up to carry the weight.

What Happens When You Sell This Way
Sellers like Elise don't close more deals because they're better talkers. They close more deals because they're trusted sooner and doubted less. They don't perform. They partner. They don't ask the buyer to believe in the product. They give the buyer reasons to believe in them.

The Room Goes Quiet

That's what Rachel remembered. Not the timeline. Not the feature set. She remembered the one person who didn't flinch when the pressure came out.

And that's the kind of presence that gets you called back, and not just for the next deal, but also for the ones that never even go to RFP.

William Anderson

Chapter 10: The Silent Advantage – Mastering Body Language & Non-Verbal Sales Cues

Sales is far more than what you say. It's what you signal. The most elite sales professionals don't just master the pitch; they master the silent game. They understand that from the moment they step into a room (or even onto a video call), they are being evaluated on a subconscious level. Every detail matters: posture, facial expressions, vocal tone, clothing choices, and the way they occupy space.

This has fascinated me for years. I've watched countless sales interactions and leadership meetings where deals were won or lost before the real discussion even started, simply because of the way one person carried themselves, dressed, moved, or reacted. The best salespeople know how to use nonverbal cues to guide conversations, build trust, and subtly reinforce their authority.

Body language isn't just about looking confident. It's about reading the room, catching micro-expressions that indicate hesitation or lack of interest, and adjusting in real time. Clothing choices aren't random. They're deliberate tools to influence perception. Even the way someone speaks, the pauses they use, their pacing, and the verbal fillers they use can either command attention or erode credibility.

Understanding these cues and mastering the ability to control them is a secret weapon in sales.

First Impressions: The 7-Second Judgment Window

Before a word is spoken, people have already formed an opinion. Research suggests it takes only seven seconds for someone to judge your competence, confidence, and intent. By

The Room Goes Quiet

the time you introduce yourself, their subconscious has already decided whether they trust you.

Most of this happens below the surface. People do not consciously think, *This person looks competent*. Instead, their brains rapidly assess nonverbal cues. Albert Mehrabian's communication model, often called the "7–38–55 rule," found that when verbal and nonverbal signals conflict, people place disproportionate weight on body language and tone:

- Body language (55%): posture, facial expressions, stance, and movement
- Tone of voice (38%): warmth, confidence, volume, and pacing
- Actual words spoken (7%): the least important element if the nonverbal cues are misaligned

If your body language contradicts your words, your words will lose every time.

A strong first impression is not about faking confidence. It is about deliberately controlling the silent messages you send. The way you walk into a room, the way you stand, and the way you shake hands all influence whether people perceive you as an authority or as someone unsure of their own value.

The strongest first impressions come from deliberate control of the following:

- Posture: Stand tall with your shoulders back and chest open. Taking up space signals confidence. Avoid small, hesitant movements that suggest insecurity.
- Eye contact: Hold eye contact for three to five seconds at a time. This is long enough to show confidence without turning it into a stare-down. Looking away too often creates subconscious doubt about your authority.

- Facial expressions: Maintain a natural, relaxed smile to appear approachable and competent. Avoid a forced smile or a blank expression, which can make you look disengaged.
- Handshake: Use a firm but controlled handshake that signals confidence. Avoid a weak grip that suggests hesitation or an overly aggressive one that feels insecure or domineering.
- Voice tone: Speak clearly with a calm and deliberate cadence. Avoid speaking too fast, which signals nervous energy, or too slow, which suggests a lack of conviction.

First impressions set the tone. If you walk in looking hesitant, the customer assumes you lack confidence. If you project certainty, they assume you belong in the room.

The Power of Positioning: Where You Stand, Sit, and Move in a Room

Sales is a game of presence, and how you position yourself within a room dictates power dynamics. Too many salespeople overlook this. They focus so much on what they're saying that they don't realize they've physically positioned themselves in a way that makes it harder to be taken seriously.

Have you ever walked into a meeting and instinctively felt that someone was on the defensive before a word was spoken? Or sat across from someone and realized that, without meaning to, you had set up a psychological opposition rather than a partnership?

Standing Position and Presence

- Standing with feet shoulder-width apart projects stability and confidence. Shifting your weight back and forth signals uncertainty.
- Keeping hands relaxed at your sides or lightly

The Room Goes Quiet

clasped in front of you projects authority. Shoving them in your pockets or fidgeting with a pen weakens your authority.

- Pacing or restless shifting makes you look anxious. Moving with intention signals confidence.

Sitting Position & Presence

One of the biggest mistakes salespeople make is sitting directly across from the customer. It creates a subconscious barrier, a subtle "me versus you" dynamic. Instead, whenever possible, sit next to them or at an angle. This shifts the interaction from opposition to collaboration. Further adjustments to sitting position include:

- Sitting slightly forward, not slouching or rigid, to signal engagement.
- Keeping both feet on the ground. Tucking them under the chair or crossing them tightly can signal discomfort or defensiveness.
- Avoiding crossing your arms, as this creates a subconscious barrier between you and the customer.

Red Flags to Watch For in Others

- If a customer leans in, they're engaged
- If they lean back with crossed arms, they're skeptical or disengaged
- If they mirror your posture, they're aligned with you mentally
- If they place an object between you, like a laptop, phone, or coffee cup, they're creating a subconscious barrier

Mastering Non-Verbal Sales

Sales is initiated before words are spoken. The hidden levers that dictate how people perceive you are posture, positioning, vocal tone, clothing, and micro-expressions.

The best salespeople own the room, whether in person or on a screen. They use presence, body language, and subconscious cues to guide the conversation before the customer even realizes it.

Words matter. But what you signal matters more.

Chapter 11: Taking Responsibility for Customer Outcomes

Committing to Transformation, Not Just Delivering Value

Success in service sales isn't about simply delivering what was promised. It's about ensuring that the customer achieves lasting transformation. The difference between a transactional service provider and a true strategic partner lies in ownership. The best providers don't see their responsibility as ending when the contract is signed. That's when it begins.

Too often, service providers confine their engagement to contractual commitments, executing only what is outlined in a statement of work. While contracts define scope, they do not define success. Customers evaluate providers based on formal agreements, but long-term partnerships are built on a provider's ability to own outcomes, proactively solve challenges, align with shifting business goals, and ensure sustained impact beyond the initial engagement.

Moving Beyond Contractual Obligations

Contractual commitments set the foundation for service delivery: timelines, deliverables, and expected outcomes. But the most successful providers move beyond this foundation, making informal commitments that drive deeper customer engagement and ongoing value.

Consider a technology services firm implementing a cloud migration for a global financial institution. The contract may specify migrating applications, ensuring security compliance, and meeting a go-live deadline. But a service provider who truly owns customer outcomes doesn't just focus on execution. They proactively anticipate post-migration challenges, support internal adoption, and provide strategic recommendations that ensure long-term success.

William Anderson

Failure to anticipate roadblocks, such as employee resistance to new systems, hidden security risks, or underestimated infrastructure complexity, can derail an otherwise successful project. A provider who takes ownership doesn't wait for problems to arise. They identify and mitigate risks before they materialize.

What separates vendors from strategic partners is a willingness to invest in customer success beyond the terms of the contract.

Measuring Success: The Customer Success Scorecard

For service providers to remain accountable for both contractual and informal commitments, they must have a structured approach to tracking and validating success. The following Customer Success Scorecard provides a framework for ensuring customer outcomes are consistently met, not just the project deliverables.

This scorecard evaluates success in three dimensions:

Dimension	Key Metrics	Evaluation Criteria
Operational Impact	System uptime, response time, issue resolution speed	Does service meet/exceed SLA commitments
Business Impact	Cost savings, productivity gains, revenue growth	Has the service driven measurable ROI
Strateegic Allignment	Customer retention, expansion, Expansion opportunities, executive advocacy	Is the provider viewed as a trusted adviser

The Room Goes Quiet

Beyond quantitative metrics, qualitative assessments such as customer sentiment, responsiveness to challenges, and alignment with evolving business objectives help create a full picture of service impact. Reviewing this scorecard with customers regularly, rather than only internally, ensures that accountability is shared between provider and customer and reinforces a culture of continuous improvement.

Situation: A Commitment Beyond the Contract

A global retail company undergoing a digital transformation engaged a consulting firm to modernize its supply chain systems. The contract outlined a twelve-month implementation timeline with specific technical milestones. However, external factors such as supply chain disruptions and shifting consumer behavior forced the company to rethink its logistics strategy midway through the project.

A transactional provider would have insisted on sticking to the original scope. Instead, the consulting firm recognized that true success required adapting to the customer's evolving reality. Rather than treating this as an out-of-scope issue, they partnered with the client to refine the integration plan, incorporate real-time inventory tracking, and introduce new predictive analytics for demand forecasting.

Had they simply delivered on the original contract, the client's new supply chain system would have been outdated before it was fully deployed. By taking ownership beyond the contract, they didn't just complete a project. They strengthened the customer's competitive advantage. As a result, the company extended its engagement with the consulting firm for ongoing advisory services, securing a long-term partnership.

Creating a Culture of Ownership

For service organizations to build a reputation for true customer commitment, ownership must be a mindset embraced at every level, from leadership to sales to delivery teams. It requires embedding a philosophy that customer success is company success and not an afterthought.

Service leaders must:

- **Train sales teams** to position engagements as long-term partnerships rather than transactions
- **Empower customer success teams** to track value beyond deliverables using structured scorecards
- **Align incentives** to reward not just deal closure but measurable customer impact
- **Encourage proactive problem-solving** so that teams anticipate customer needs and provide solutions before issues arise

Embedding these principles into daily operations ensures that customers see their service provider not as a vendor, but as a strategic ally who actively works toward their success.

Becoming a Trusted Partner Beyond the Sale

Customers prefer to work with providers who don't just sell solutions but own the success of those solutions. The service professionals who stay engaged beyond the initial contract, solve problems before they escalate, and continuously provide strategic guidance become indispensable partners.

Success in service sales isn't measured by the number of contracts signed. It's measured by the customers who achieve real transformation and choose to re-engage. By implementing a customer success scorecard, committing to accountability beyond the contract, and fostering a culture of ownership, service leaders position themselves as true business partners.

The question is not "Did we deliver what was promised?" but rather "Did we ensure the customer achieved meaningful success?" By prioritizing both, service providers move from being vendors to becoming essential, long-term partners.

The Room Goes Quiet

Case Study: The Power of a Well-Timed Success Story

The Setup: Turning Hesitation into Confidence

This deal had been dragging.

We had been in discussions for months with a mid-sized manufacturing company, working to help them modernize their factory floor operations. Their existing system was outdated, manual, and costing them efficiency. Their maintenance teams were constantly reacting to equipment failures instead of predicting them, which led to unplanned downtime, missed production targets, and frustrated leadership.

The problem was clear. The pain was real.

But they weren't moving forward.

I had been speaking with David, the vice president of operations, who liked the idea but wasn't convinced it was worth the investment. He understood the value in theory, but I could tell he wasn't feeling the urgency. Every time we got close to pushing the deal forward, he pulled back.

"What if the ROI isn't there?" he asked. "We've been doing things this way for a long time. How do I know this will actually work for us?"

David wasn't looking for more data or another proposal slide. He needed something more tangible. Something that made him believe.

That was when I knew it was time for a story.

Framing the Story: Making It Relatable

I paused for a moment and leaned in slightly, lowering my voice just enough to signal that what I was about to say wasn't just another pitch.

"David, I worked with another company in your industry that had almost the exact same concerns."

He stopped looking at his notepad and made eye contact with me. That was the first time in the conversation that he was truly locked in.

"They had been running on a manual maintenance system for years," I continued. "The plant manager told me the same thing you just did: 'We've been doing it this way forever, and it works well enough.' They were skeptical, too."

I let that sink in for a second before moving on. I wasn't throwing more statistics at him. I was setting up a situation that mirrored his own experience, letting him place himself in the story.

"But here's what happened," I said. "In their first six months after implementing predictive maintenance, they reduced unplanned downtime by 32 percent. One of their biggest issues was a bottleneck on their assembly line due to unexpected equipment failures. With predictive alerts, they scheduled maintenance before issues became failures. That one change alone saved them hundreds of hours in lost production time."

David's posture shifted. He wasn't just hearing me now. He was seeing the possibilities.

"What really made them believers," I continued, "was when they avoided a major breakdown that would have shut down production for three days. That event alone paid for the entire investment in the first year."

I let the silence hang for a second. Then I asked the most important question.

"What would a 32 percent reduction in unplanned downtime

The Room Goes Quiet

mean for your team?"

Why It Worked: The Psychology Behind Success Stories

David didn't hesitate this time. "It would be huge," he said, shaking his head slightly as if the numbers were still settling in his mind. "We lose thousands of hours every year to downtime. If we could get ahead of that . . . it would change everything."

That was the turning point.

I could have answered his ROI question with spreadsheets and projections. I could have walked him through hypothetical cost-savings scenarios. But what made the difference was giving him a real-world, concrete example of success, one that felt tangible, relatable, and believable.

Stories work in sales because they bypass skepticism and activate the imagination. Instead of trying to convince someone logically, they allow the listener to see themselves in the experience.

I hadn't told David that this investment was worth it. I had let him draw that conclusion himself.

Closing the Deal: Momentum Through Confidence

By the end of the conversation, David was asking different questions.

He wasn't focused on whether it would work. He was focused on how soon they could get started.

"What does the implementation timeline look like?"

"How do we make sure our team is ready for the transition?"

Within a few weeks, we had finalized the agreement.

What Went Well: Why This Story Landed at the Right Time

This wasn't just about telling a story. It was about telling the right story at the right moment.

It worked because it was relevant. I didn't just share a generic success story. I picked a case that mirrored his industry, his challenges, and his concerns.

It was specific but not overloaded. The story had just enough detail to feel real but wasn't bogged down with unnecessary facts.

It painted a clear before-and-after picture. I didn't focus on features but on transformation. What life was like before, and what changed after.

It ended with a guiding question. Instead of saying, "This could work for you too," I asked, "What would this mean for your team?" That shifted the conversation from an abstract concept to a personal realization.

Lesson: When Logic Fails, Stories Win

Customers don't just buy services. They buy confidence.

And confidence isn't built through data alone. It's built through trust, belief, and real-world proof.

A well-timed success story does more than explain. It lets the customer step into the shoes of someone who has already leaped. It makes the risk feel smaller, the outcome feel inevitable, and the investment feel like the right decision.

That's why the best salespeople aren't just experts in solutions.

They're expert storytellers.

The Room Goes Quiet

Chapter 12: Reframing Risk – Turning Buyer Hesitation into Forward Motion

In B2B sales, we tell ourselves that logic and reason rule the day. Executives, we believe, make decisions based on ROI models, strategic alignment, and technical fit. But if that were true, why do so many well-scoped, properly priced deals stall anyway?

Because numbers don't close deals, people do. And people are driven by emotion more than they admit.

What looks like hesitation is often something deeper. It's not about your pricing model, your feature set, or even your references. It's about *fear*. It's about *confidence*. And it's about the most human of decision-making drivers: *risk aversion*.

Fear: The Unspoken Obstacle

Fear is the most reliable deal killer in sales. It rarely shows up in conversation, but it always shows up in behavior:

- Delays and reschedules with no clear reason
- Last-minute approvals added to the process
- Fixation on irrelevant contract language

These aren't due diligence steps; they're signs of a buyer who's scared to say yes.

Imagine a CIO sitting across from you, arms crossed. They've seen initiatives like yours crash and burn. They don't fear your service. They fear what it means for *them* if it doesn't go right.

How to overcome fear:

- Reframe the risk: What happens if they *don't* act?

Who's already ahead?

- Prove it's safe: Show examples from similar companies and successful outcomes
- Reduce perceived danger: Break initiatives into manageable phases with clear milestones

Seller: "We've outlined the ROI. What's holding us back?"

Buyer: "I just want to make sure we've explored every option."

Translation: "I'm afraid of making the wrong call and getting blamed if it fails."

Confidence: The Hidden Currency of Buying Decisions

Confidence transfers. If you're tentative, buyers will be too. If you speak with clarity, resolve, and a command of your solution's value, they'll borrow your certainty.

Hesitation sounds like:

- "Let me check with a few more people"
- "Let's revisit this next quarter"
- "We just need more data before deciding"

Each one signals a lack of internal conviction. You haven't lost the deal, but you haven't won belief.

How to build confidence:

- Master your message: Speak with clarity and avoid hedge language
- Preempt objections: Address risks proactively and don't wait to be asked
- Lead with insight: Bring something the buyer didn't know

The Room Goes Quiet

Seller: "Sounds like you see the potential here. How do you feel about championing this internally?"

Buyer: "I believe in it . . . but I need to check with a few more people."

Translation: "I'm not confident enough to risk my reputation. Yet."

Risk Aversion: The Silent Deal Killer

Executives rarely choose the *best* option. They choose the *safest* one.

Even mediocre incumbents survive longer than they should, simply because they're familiar. Familiarity lowers perceived risk. And in B2B, familiarity often beats better.

Red flags of risk aversion:

- Obsession with existing systems: "It's not perfect, but it works"
- Hyperfocus on comparisons: Feature-by-feature competitions that delay decisions
- No discussion of implementation: A refusal to talk about next steps equals avoidance of change

How to overcome risk aversion:

- Normalize the change: Use examples from others who've transitioned successfully
- Provide a clear roadmap: Eliminate ambiguity with a detailed rollout plan
- Identify internal advocates: Empower them to de-risk the decision from within

Seller: "This will reduce costs significantly."

William Anderson

Buyer: "Sure, but we've used this system for years, and it works."

Translation: "I'd rather deal with inefficiency than face the unknown."

Selling to the Real Decision-Maker: Emotion

No matter how senior the title is, every buyer is still a person. And every person wants three things when making a business decision:

- To avoid looking foolish
- To feel in control
- To make the *safe* call

Your job isn't just to explain what you're selling. It's to quiet their fear, to strengthen their confidence, and to make the risk of doing nothing greater than the risk of saying yes.

The Room Goes Quiet

Chapter 13: The Risk Ownership Framework: Four Pillars of Service Sales

Stories open eyes. Frameworks change behavior. In high-stakes selling, you need both. The stories in this book will stay with you, but the framework is what you'll use when the pressure is real and the silence stretches. This isn't for your customer. It's for you.

Executives remember models. So should you. A framework is a mental map you carry into the room. It keeps you from getting pulled off course by personalities, politics, or pressure. When the room goes quiet, this is what steadies you.

I once watched a seller do nearly everything right. They broke through the executive's skepticism and earned real trust. They named the risks, even the uncomfortable ones, and won respect for it. They held firm when the customer pressed for concessions, structuring the deal with discipline. For a moment, the win felt inevitable. But weeks later the deal died quietly. Not because of price, not because of delivery doubts. It died in the retelling. The champion didn't have the language to carry the story up the chain. The seller built trust, owned risk, showed discipline—but they never gave the buyer a way to scale the value. One pillar missing, and the structure collapsed.

That's why this framework matters. Every deal you've read about—or lived through—comes back to four pillars. They aren't abstract theories. They are the foundation of service sales. Miss one, and you feel the weakness. Strengthen all four, and you can hold the weight of the biggest deal in the building.

The Four Pillars of Service Sales

- Trust Building: Everything starts here. Without trust, your expertise is background noise. Building trust is not small talk or charm. It's showing that you see

what others miss—the hesitation in a question, the guarded tone when money comes up, the risk no one else is naming. Trust is earned when the buyer realizes you'll say the thing everyone else avoids
Mantra: Trust is built in signals, not slides

- Risk Ownership: Every service sale is built on risk. Pretend it isn't there and you'll sound like every vendor hiding behind fine print. Own it and you separate yourself immediately. Owning risk does not mean reckless promises. It means standing shoulder to shoulder with the buyer and saying, "This is what's at stake. Here's what I'll carry with you." That's the moment you stop sounding transactional and start sounding indispensable
Mantra: Risk avoided is risk amplified. Name it

- Execution Discipline: The room tests you. When silence follows a demand, weak sellers fold. Discipline is what keeps you from conceding. Execution discipline means structuring commitments and trading value, not giving it away. It is the line between confidence and desperation. This is where deals are either secured or surrendered
Mantra: Discipline means trading, not conceding

- Scaling Value: Even if you win the room, the deal won't hold unless the value travels. Scaling value is making sure your story doesn't die when your champion repeats it to a skeptical CFO or a restless board. You arm them with language, proof, and clarity so they can extend your voice when you're not there. Without it, momentum stops at the door
Mantra: A story that doesn't travel dies where it was told

You don't need complexity. You need clarity. Four pillars. Trust. Risk. Execution. Scale. Simple enough to sketch on a napkin. Strong enough to carry through the toughest deal.

Make It Yours

The Room Goes Quiet

As you move through the rest of this book, tie every story back to these four pillars. Ask yourself: Which one held? Which one cracked? Where would I have stumbled? Use the framework as your filter. The more you practice it, the more automatic it becomes. That's how you move from reading about deals to mastering your own.

Turning Trust into Execution

Trust is the foundation of service sales, but trust alone does not close deals or drive long-term success. The organizations that thrive are the ones that recognize trust as an asset that must be reinforced through execution. A customer may believe in your expertise, but without clear execution strategies, that belief can quickly turn into hesitation, or worse, disengagement.

Building trust is not the goal; it is the starting point. The real challenge is ensuring that trust translates into structured action, risk mitigation, and measurable success. Without execution, even the strongest customer relationships can stall or fall apart.

In the next section, we will explore:

- Structuring deals for long-term business impact
- Managing risk while maintaining customer confidence
- Turning stalled deals into momentum-driven success
- Strengthening multilevel influence to align decision-makers and end users

Trust alone won't close the deal. It's time to execute.

William Anderson

Part III: Execution—From Strategy to Success

Chapter 14: Qualifying Opportunities Through Collaboration & Strategic Positioning

Moving from Vendor to Indispensable Partner

A mid-sized healthcare provider was struggling to keep up with evolving compliance regulations. Their systems were outdated, vulnerable to fines, and slowing down patient care. Vendors lined up with slide decks full of features, but none of them stuck.

Except one.

Rather than leading with technology, one provider opened with a story. A similar organization had reduced compliance violations by 70 percent. The seller didn't just sell capability; they sold certainty. By the end of the meeting, the conversation had shifted. Pricing wasn't the focus. They wanted to know how soon they could begin.

This is the shift at the heart of service sales. Buyers are no longer making choices based on features. They're evaluating who understands their business, can anticipate risk, and show evidence of impact. They don't want a vendor. They want a partner who's already walked this path.

This sets the stage for a deeper transformation in the sales process. One where the provider earns a place at the table not by presenting, but by collaborating. Not by pitching, but by solving.

Collaborative Qualification Begins Before the First Conversation

In modern service sales, positioning doesn't begin in the meeting but long before that. Buyers are educated. By the time they engage, they've researched competitors, read case studies, and formed initial opinions. They don't want to be taught what's possible. They want someone who already understands what's probable.

Take the consultant who regularly publishes insights tailored to operational challenges in manufacturing. When a plant manager came across their article on reducing downtime through predictive maintenance, the decision was already tilting. The seller didn't have to earn attention in the room; they had already earned authority before stepping into it.

Credibility now precedes contact. Influence is built by showing value in advance. The most effective positioning happens when the buyer sees your expertise at work before you ever speak a word.

From Positioning to Qualification: Creating Fit Through Co-Creation

Positioning might open the door, but qualification determines whether you walk through it together. The traditional approach treats qualification as a checkpoint to see if the customer is ready to buy. But in service sales, qualification is a shared assessment of whether both parties are the right fit to solve a complex problem together.

This mutual discovery starts with defining the business challenge. Until both sides are clear on the root cause, no solution will land cleanly. Once there is clarity, the conversation moves to desired outcomes and shared definitions of success. From there, you can build a roadmap together, one that charts how success will be achieved, measured, and sustained.

Qualification, when done collaboratively, becomes less about filters and more about alignment. It's not about saying yes or no. It's about deciding together whether this is a problem worth solving and whether this partnership is the right one to solve it.

The Room Goes Quiet

Conversational Mastery: Moving from Pitching to Guiding

Strategic positioning builds presence. Collaborative qualification builds connection. But the glue between the two is how you engage in conversation.

Salespeople who default to scripted pitches lose the opportunity to learn what matters. The best elevate the dialogue with open-ended, exploratory questions that unlock real insight. Instead of asking, "Would you like to see a demo?" ask, "What's made this challenge hard to solve before?" Instead of saying, "Can we walk you through our approach?" ask, "What would success look like in the first ninety days?"

These are not tricks. They are invitations. Invitations for the buyer to take ownership of the conversation and co-author the solution. When buyers speak their goals out loud, they begin internalizing them. When they define success in their own words, they're more likely to pursue it.

And when the service provider facilitates this journey, trust is built, not through persuasion, but through participation.

The Cost of Getting It Wrong

This cautionary tale reminds us of what's at stake. A provider landed a major contract with a healthcare system to implement a new patient data platform. The technology was strong. The IT team was on board. But the sales team never engaged with compliance or clinical operations during qualification.

Six months later, the project unraveled. Compliance flagged major gaps with the Health Insurance Portability and Accountability Act (HIPAA). Clinicians rejected the interface as clunky and disruptive. Frustration grew. Timelines slipped. Trust eroded.

Had the sales team brought these stakeholders into the qualification process early and co-defined success across departments, the roadblocks could have been addressed before they became liabilities. Instead, the provider was forced to eat costs, extend timelines, and claw its way back from lost credibility.

This is why collaborative qualification isn't just a sales tactic. It's a risk-mitigation strategy. When customers help shape the plan, they're more likely to support it. When they're left out, they become the resistance.

Joint Discovery Sessions: Designing the Future Together

One of the most powerful tools in this approach is the joint discovery session. These sessions are not about pitching solutions. They are about designing them together.

A joint discovery session opens with alignment around the problem. Not a rehash of the customer's slides, but a real dialogue to confirm what's broken and why it matters. From there, the conversation explores desired outcomes, co-defines success criteria, and examines multiple ways to get there. The goal is not to steer the buyer to your offering. The goal is to explore possibilities openly and without pressure.

By the time the session ends, both sides should feel they've created something together. That co-creation is what accelerates buy-in. It's also what shortens the sales cycle. Because when customers help build the plan, they don't second-guess it. They drive it forward.

Social Proof Isn't a Slide: It's a Signal

Buyers carry risk. Not just financial, but reputational. A nervous buyer once said, "We want to do something bold, but no one wants to be the first to fall." That's the real fear in many service deals. Not failure. Exposure.

A smart team once helped a regional telco consolidate three legacy systems. They reduced outages by 40 percent. But

The Room Goes Quiet

instead of tucking that story away in a capabilities deck, they led every new conversation with it.

They didn't just share the success. They framed it as reassurance.

"You don't have to bet blind. Here's what this looked like for another operations lead who faced the same risk curve you're on."

That's when trust shifts. Not because of the metric. Because the buyer feels less alone.

Social proof works best when it speaks directly to the buyer's world. When it shows what it's like to succeed through fear, uncertainty, and doubt. It becomes less about bragging and more about backing up the buyer's decision with relevance they can feel.

Scarcity Reframes the Power Dynamic

Some firms struggle because they're always available. Always responsive. Always trying to be chosen.

But power in service sales often shifts when a firm becomes selective. One company changed their posture. Instead of saying "We're ready whenever you are," they said:

"We take on only two transformation clients per quarter because our senior team stays engaged from scoping through adoption. That's the only way we ensure outcomes."

It wasn't posturing. It was executional discipline. But it transformed how buyers responded. Timelines accelerated. Internal champions became advocates. Scarcity shifted urgency from the seller's side to the buyer's.

When you position your services as intentional, high-impact, and selective, buyers stop evaluating your price and start fighting for your time. That's the power of positioning rooted in value and not in volume.

The Path from Strategic Positioning to Execution

Positioning earns attention. Qualification earns trust. Joint discovery earns commitment. But none of it matters if you don't deliver.

The sales process doesn't end when the contract is signed. It culminates when the customer sees the outcomes they were promised. That's why the best sales teams work hand-in-hand with delivery from the beginning. They set realistic expectations. They identify internal blockers. They prepare the customer not just to buy, but to succeed.

When service providers position themselves as indispensable, collaborate to qualify opportunities, and anchor each interaction in relevance and respect, they build more than pipeline. They build momentum.

And momentum, once earned, turns potential into performance.

Case Study: The Champion Who Wasn't a Decision-Maker

The Setup: A Sales Process Built on Assumptions

This deal had all the makings of a win. The customer, a mid-sized technology services firm, was struggling with inefficiencies in its IT service management platform. Their support teams were overwhelmed with manual processes and response times that were lagging behind industry standards, and internal complaints about system bottlenecks were piling up.

We had been working closely with Jake, a senior manager in IT operations, who had been vocal about the need for change. He had firsthand experience with the pain points, understood the technical limitations of their current system, and had been the one raising the issue internally for months. His team was under constant pressure to resolve tickets faster, yet they were stuck dealing with outdated workflows that forced them to triage and escalate issues manually.

From our first few meetings, it was clear that Jake saw the value in what we were proposing. He was engaged in discussions, asked thoughtful technical questions, and pushed for details on implementation. When we walked him through the impact that automation and predictive analytics could have on his team's workload, his response was immediate.

"This is exactly what we need," Jake said, leaning forward. "I know my boss is aligned. Let me take this to her, and we should be good to move forward."

He said it with confidence, as if this were simply a matter of moving the process along. There was no hesitation in his voice, no hedging or uncertainty. He had been the one pushing for a solution, and now that he had found it, he was eager to get leadership on board.

We took that as a strong buying signal.

What we didn't realize was that Jake was not the person who could approve this deal, and more importantly, he wasn't equipped to sell it internally.

The First Breakdown: Lost in Translation to the Senior Director

Two weeks later, we followed up with Jake, expecting good news.

"My boss, Aisha, the senior director, likes it," he said. "But she wants to understand the cost structure better before we finalize things."

That was our first red flag.

We had spent hours walking Jake through not just the cost, but the total value: how the investment would reduce support ticket resolution times, how automation would free up their engineers, and how long-term savings would offset upfront costs.

The fact that cost was now the focus instead of value told us one thing: Jake had explained the proposal, but he hadn't communicated the real impact.

Before we went into the meeting with Aisha, I checked in with Lisa, our account executive.

"Jake told us Aisha is on board, but I just want to make sure we're aligned before we go into this," I said.

Lisa waved away the concern. "Aisha and I talk all the time," she assured me. "She's sharp, and if she says she's aligned, she's aligned."

When we got on the call with Aisha, it became clear that it wasn't entirely true.

Aisha wasn't disengaged, but she wasn't fully locked in either.

The Room Goes Quiet

She was polite, nodding along as we explained the business impact of the engagement, but her questions were surface-level and focused on logistics, not value.

"Can you remind me what's included in the baseline package?"

"Is this something that would require ongoing maintenance from our side?"

"How does this compare to what we have today?"

All reasonable questions, but not the questions of someone who was actively weighing the impact of the solution. These were the questions of someone who wasn't convinced there was a real problem to solve yet.

I tried pressing a little.

"Aisha, does this align with what you're trying to accomplish this year? What's the biggest concern on your side?"

She hesitated for just a second before responding.

"I mean, I see where this could be helpful," she said. "But at the end of the day, we're making a lot of investments, and this is one of several priorities. We'll have to see what leadership thinks."

Something about the way she said it felt off. There was no urgency, no acknowledgment of the problem we were solving, just a pass-off to the next level.

We left the call uneasy, but Lisa reassured us.

"Aisha is careful with her words," she said. "If she says she'll bring it to the VP, she will."

We took her word for it. That was our mistake.

The Second Breakdown: The VP Never Heard the Real Value

Two more weeks passed with no word.

When we finally reached Jake, he sounded discouraged.

"Aisha took it to the VP," he told us. "And she wasn't convinced. She doesn't see why we need this right now."

We pushed for a meeting with Aisha.

When we got on the call, she seemed annoyed.

"I explained the proposal," she said, "but leadership didn't see the urgency. They're asking why we need to spend this much when our current system still works."

That was when it hit us. Aisha had never fully understood the value in the first place, and now she had to explain it to someone with even less context.

The senior vice president, the real decision-maker, hadn't heard anything about:

- How automation would reduce ticket resolution times by 40%
- How their engineers were spending twenty-plus hours a week on manual tasks that our solution would eliminate
- How customer satisfaction scores were dropping due to slow response times

Instead, she had told them:

"They want us to spend money on a platform upgrade, but I think we're fine with what we have for now."

We finally got a meeting with the VP, and within five minutes of walking her through the real value of the proposal, she stopped us.

The Room Goes Quiet

"If that's how it was explained to me initially, I would absolutely buy this," she said.

That statement stuck with me.

The problem had never been that leadership wasn't interested. It was that they had never actually heard a strong case for the investment.

But by the time we had this conversation, it was too late.

"I get it now," the VP continued, "but I've already told finance we're not moving forward. If I go back now and say we need to do this, I lose credibility. We'll have to look at this again next year."

Four months of effort, gone.

What We Should Have Done Differently

The mistake wasn't just relying on Jake, but assuming each level of leadership was effectively selling the idea to the next one.

What we should have done:

- Instead of just asking "Do you understand?" we should have asked "How would you explain this to your leadership?"
- Before letting Aisha take it to the VP, we should have role-played her pitch. "What do you think your VP will ask about? How are you planning to position this?"
- We should have pushed for earlier access to the leadership. "Since this is a strategic decision, would it make sense for us to have a direct conversation with your VP? We want to make sure we align with their priorities."

William Anderson

Lesson: Never Assume Your Champion Can Sell for You

Customers don't buy services. They buy outcomes.

And if the decision-makers never hear the **real case for the outcome**, the deal is lost before it even reaches them. It's not enough to assume our message is getting through. We have to confirm at every level that the right people understand it well enough to act on it.

Otherwise, we aren't just losing the deal. We're never actually in the deal to begin with.

Chapter 15: Risk Management & Deal Governance – From Mitigation to Strategic Advantage

The meeting was going well until the topic of risk came up.

The sales team had covered everything: ROI projections, technical capabilities, and implementation timelines. They had the key decision-makers engaged, nodding along, asking the right questions. The deal felt within reach.

Then, the CFO leaned forward.

"Before we move forward, tell me this: what happens if this fails?"

The energy in the room shifted. The sales lead hesitated. They had plenty of answers about mitigation strategies and contingency plans, but that wasn't really what the CFO was asking.

"I'm not asking about your process," she clarified. "I'm asking what happens to us and who takes responsibility when things don't go as planned?"

The silence that followed lasted only a few seconds, but it was enough. The trust they had built was starting to unravel.

Later during the internal debrief, the regional sales VP summed it up.

"That was the moment we lost the deal. Not because we didn't have a plan, but because we couldn't prove we owned the risk."

The full details of this deal, and how it unraveled, were covered earlier, but this moment highlights a critical failure in how most service sales teams approach risk. It's not enough to identify potential risks. Customers expect their providers to own them.

The Hidden Cost of Poor Risk Management

A senior executive at a consulting firm recalls a deal that unraveled for similar reasons.

"We were six months into a digital transformation project. Everything looked good on paper. Green status reports. On-budget metrics. Then the client's CFO called."

He pauses, shaking his head.

"She asked one question: 'Do you know our SAP upgrade is scheduled for the same weekend as your platform migration?' We didn't. Nobody had mapped the dependencies. That oversight cost us $4 million in emergency resources and nearly destroyed a decade-long relationship."

This kind of scenario happens every day. Service providers invest enormous effort in winning deals but often treat risk as a delivery problem: something for project teams to figure out later.

A risk officer at a major technology services firm sees this play out constantly.

"Most sales teams get it backward. They think risk management slows down deals. But the best teams use it to win. They own the risks better than anyone else, and that gives customers confidence."

From Reactive to Strategic: The Evolution of Risk Management

A consultant who has spent years turning around troubled engagements is direct about the issue.

"Everyone has a risk management framework. They have their

The Room Goes Quiet

matrixes, their heat maps, their mitigation plans. But most of them are useless because they're designed to check boxes, not prevent failures."

He recalls a recent deal where two firms competed for a $30 million cloud transformation contract.

The first firm presented a standard risk assessment, a detailed matrix covering technical, operational, and financial risks.

The second firm took a different approach. They didn't just identify risks, but walked the client through three failure scenarios:

- A complete transformation failure
- A technical success with poor user adoption
- A successful but significantly delayed implementation

For each scenario, they mapped out the financial impact, the operational disruptions, and, most importantly, exactly what they would do if it happened.

"The first firm showed they understood risks," he explains. "The second firm showed they owned them. The difference wasn't in their capabilities. It was in their mindset."

The Ownership Framework: A New Approach to Risk

A senior partner at a consulting firm learned this lesson the hard way after losing a $15 million deal.

"We had the best solution, the strongest team, and a competitive price. But in the final presentation, the client's CEO asked each vendor one question: 'What happens if this fails?'"

The competitor's response changed everything.

"They didn't try to downplay the risks. They embraced them and walked through exactly what would happen: the financial impact, the operational disruption, and the reputational damage. Then they showed their prevention strategy, their recovery plan, and, most importantly, how much of their own money they were willing to put at risk."

That deal was lost, but the lesson transformed their approach. They developed what they now call the Ownership Framework, a way of evaluating and presenting risk that shifts the conversation from mitigation to ownership.

It starts with three core questions:

- What's the worst thing that could happen?
- What's the most likely thing to go wrong?
- What don't we know that we should?

"But here's the key," he explains. "We don't just identify risks. We own them. For every major risk, we specify exactly what we'll do if it happens and how much it will cost us, and not the client."

Governance That Works

A sales executive recalls how her company nearly lost a major deal—not because of the risks themselves, but because of how they handled governance.

"We had fourteen approval steps, three committees, and a pricing board. By the time we got through all of it, our customer had moved on."

That experience forced them to rethink how governance should function in service sales.

"Traditional governance tries to eliminate risk. That's impossible. The goal isn't to eliminate risk. It's to understand it well enough to price it and own it properly."

The Room Goes Quiet

She developed a model called Active Governance, which puts ownership at the center of every decision. Instead of asking, "Should we do this deal?" the process now asks, "Are we willing to own the consequences if this goes wrong?"

This shift changed everything. Governance meetings became decision-focused instead of compliance exercises. Deal reviews now center around three critical questions:

- Do we understand what could go wrong?
- Are we capable of preventing or handling those scenarios?
- Are we willing to put our money behind that capability?

"The interesting thing," she notes, "is that we're actually taking on bigger risks than before. But because we understand them better and price them properly, our success rate has gone up dramatically."

This mindset shift, from risk avoidance to risk monetization, doesn't just influence deal velocity. It repositions the service provider from a delivery vendor to a strategic partner. Governance becomes less about approval and more about ownership readiness. This is where the four pillars intersect: trust built through accountability, value translated into downside protection, influence earned through candor, and urgency driven by the clarity of risk.

Making the Go/No-Go Decision

A sales leader faced the toughest decision of his career when a $50 million opportunity landed on his desk. The team wanted it badly. The revenue would make their year. But something felt off.

"The tech specs were clear. The price was right. The client was enthusiastic. But when I asked what would happen if we missed the go-live date, nobody had a good answer."

He made the call to walk away. Three months later, they learned their competitor had won the deal and was now facing $10 million in penalties for missing critical milestones.

"That's when I developed my three-part test for go/no-go decisions," he explains.

1. Do we understand the real risks, not just the obvious ones?
2. Can we control or mitigate those risks?
3. Are we willing to bet our money, not just our time, on our ability to handle them?

The Future of Risk Management

The most successful service organizations today don't see risk management as a separate function. It's embedded into every aspect of the sales process. The best teams lead with risk, using it to differentiate their proposals and build credibility with customers.

A leader who pioneered this approach at her firm puts it simply.

"In today's market, the ability to understand, articulate, and own risk is more valuable than technical expertise. Anyone can do the work. The winners are the ones willing to guarantee the outcome."

The future belongs to firms that turn risk from a liability into an advantage. It's not enough to acknowledge risks. You have to own them.

The question isn't whether you can identify risks. It's whether you're willing to stake your reputation on them.

Strategic risk ownership isn't a compliance exercise; it's a credibility move. When a sales team proactively surfaces potential failure scenarios, quantifies their impact, and clearly states how they will respond, they aren't just mitigating risk.

The Room Goes Quiet

They're making a promise. And promises, when made credibly and owned publicly, build trust faster than any proof point or reference slide ever could.

Chapter 16: Value Translation – When Numbers Tell the Story

The director of operations leaned back in his chair, flipping through the proposal with a furrowed brow.

"I understand the solution," he said. "What I don't understand is why it costs three times more than doing this internally. Show me where the value is."

The sales team launched into their standard response: talking about best practices, accelerated timelines, and reduced risk. But the director wasn't having it.

"Stop," he said. "I don't need concepts. I need numbers. What's this worth in real dollars? If I put three million into this project, what do I get back? When? And how certain are you?"

The room fell silent. It was a moment that plays out daily in service sales: when good solutions fail because their value isn't translated into language decision-makers can act on.

The Value Translation Crisis

A sales leader remembers the deal that changed how she thought about value. Her firm was pitching a major digital transformation project to a manufacturing company. The solution was solid. The approach was proven. But they were stuck in procurement limbo.

"We had been going back and forth for weeks," she recalls. "Our executive sponsor believed in the project, but he couldn't get it through finance. Every time he presented it, they pushed back on the cost."

Then she had a breakthrough. Instead of talking about the transformation program, she rebuilt the entire business case

The Room Goes Quiet

from the perspective of the operations and finance teams.

"We mapped every cost center that would be impacted. We modeled the efficiency gains in their terms: cost per transaction, inventory carrying costs, and working capital impact. When we showed how a 10 percent improvement in processing time would free up $12 million in working capital, suddenly price wasn't the issue anymore."

From Features to Financials

A consultant learned this lesson the hard way after losing a $5 million consulting deal he was certain they should have won.

"The client's response changed everything," he says. "The IT director told me, 'Your solution was probably better than what we chose. But I couldn't defend the investment. The other firm showed me exactly how much money we'd save, when we'd save it, and what we could do with those savings. You showed me features.'"

That conversation led him to develop what he calls the Financial Translation Framework. At its core was a simple idea: every capability had to be expressed in financial terms.

"We stopped talking about faster deployment and started talking about the cost of delay. Instead of improved efficiency, we showed the dollar value of every percentage point improvement. We turned technical benefits into financial outcomes."

The Money Story

An enterprise sales leader recalls the first time she truly understood the power of financial translation. She was working with a telecommunications company on a massive customer service transformation.

"We had the best solution by far," she says. "But we were about to lose to a competitor who, frankly, couldn't deliver what we could. Then my VP of sales asked me a question that changed everything: 'What's the money story?'"

That question transformed their approach. Instead of leading with their solution's capabilities, they started with the financial narrative.

First, they quantified the cost of the status quo: $42 million annually in customer churn, support inefficiencies, and lost revenue opportunities. Then they mapped how their solution would impact each of these areas, showing the exact financial benefit of every improvement.

"The turning point came when we showed them that every day of delay was costing them $115,000 in lost benefits," she says. "Suddenly, their urgency to move forward matched ours."

The ROI Reality Check
A senior revenue strategist I worked with once shared an insight that has stuck with me ever since.

"Whenever I evaluate a sales team, the first thing I ask is, 'Show me your ROI model.'"

He laughed as he recalled the responses he usually got.

"Nine times out of ten, they show me something that would get laughed out of any finance review. These models are packed with aggressive assumptions, vague productivity claims, and unverified cost savings. No wonder they can't get deals approved."

He told me about a team that was struggling to sell a $2 million automation solution. Their ROI model showed a 300 percent return in the first year. On paper, it looked like an easy sell until you started asking basic questions.

"Where did this productivity improvement come from? How did you calculate the cost savings? What's the confidence level in

The Room Goes Quiet

these estimates?"

The team had no real answers. Their numbers were built on optimism rather than hard data. And then he asked the question that no one on the team saw coming:

"If this investment is really this good, if it's truly delivering a 300 percent return, then why aren't we doing it ourselves as a business? Why wouldn't we just invest in this internally, make the savings, and then resell the results?"

The room went quiet.

"That's the moment when the reality of their model hit them," he told me. "If your ROI is so good that it sounds too good to be true, it probably is. If you're claiming an impact so massive that the company should reorganize itself around this investment, you need to be ready to explain why they haven't already done so or why you haven't done it yourself."

He walked the team through a different approach. Instead of leading with their solution's benefits, they started with the customer's financial statements. They mapped every cost center that would be impacted, built conservative estimates based on real operational data, and most importantly, showed their work.

"When you can walk an operations director or finance leader through exactly how you arrived at your numbers, something shifts," he explained. "They stop questioning your conclusions and start engaging with your assumptions. That's when you know you've crossed from selling to consulting."

That conversation reshaped how I thought about ROI in service sales. If your numbers don't hold up to the question, "Why wouldn't we just do this as our business?" then they probably won't hold up in front of a CFO either. It's not about showing the biggest possible ROI. It's about making the numbers real, logical, and defensible to the people making the financial decision.

Building Cases That Convert

A senior sales leader faced a common problem. Her team's business cases weren't getting approved. The solutions were solid, the pricing was competitive, but something wasn't clicking with financial decision-makers.

"We were building cases the way we always had," she explains. "Technical benefits, efficiency gains, and risk reduction. But when these got to the finance team, they died."

She brought in a specialist in financial modeling for complex services. His assessment was blunt.

"Your business cases are built for technologists, not financial officers."

Together, they developed what she calls the Financial First approach to business cases. Every case had to answer five questions from a purely financial perspective:

- What's the real cost of the current state? Not just obvious costs, but hidden ones like opportunity cost and risk exposure.
- What's the fully loaded cost of implementing the solution?
- What's the timeline for benefits realization?
- What's the confidence level in these numbers?
- What happens to the customer's key financial metrics?

The results were immediate. Approval rates for their business cases *doubled*. But more importantly, the nature of their conversations with customers changed.

The Room Goes Quiet

"We stopped having technical discussions interrupted by financial objections," she notes. "Instead, we were having financial discussions supported by technical capabilities."

The Future of Value Translation

The question isn't whether your solution delivers value.

It's whether you can prove it in terms that drive financial decisions.

William Anderson

Chapter 17: Turning Conversations into Commitments

The Role of Strategic Conversations in Service Sales

In service sales, conversations are not just a means of communication; they are the foundation of trust, influence, and long-term success. Every interaction with a customer presents an opportunity to reinforce value, strengthen alignment, and drive progress toward shared goals. Strategic conversations go beyond surface-level discussions. They uncover deep customer motivations, align multiple stakeholders, and establish the service provider as an indispensable partner.

A well-structured conversation ensures that customers not only understand the value of a service but also become invested in its success. The most effective sales professionals integrate consistency and social proof into their discussions, making every exchange a step toward solidifying long-term engagement.

Reinforcing Commitment Through Consistency

People are more likely to follow through on commitments when they have already taken small steps toward a larger decision. This psychological principle, known as consistency, can be leveraged in service sales to create a structured path toward engagement. When customers verbalize their priorities and acknowledge their needs, they are more likely to stay committed to solutions aligned with those priorities.

A strategic conversation should begin with identifying the customer's key challenges and objectives. When a decision-maker expresses concern about operational inefficiencies, asking, "Would you agree that improving efficiency is critical to your team's success?" reinforces their own commitment to addressing the issue. As the discussion progresses, reflecting on earlier statements helps keep the customer engaged, for instance, by reminding them, "Earlier, you mentioned that system downtime was a major issue. What would it mean for

The Room Goes Quiet

your business if we could reduce that by 30 percent?" This keeps the conversation moving toward an inevitable decision point.

Customers who consistently affirm their priorities and see alignment between their challenges and the service provider's offering are far less likely to disengage or stall the decision-making process. By using this approach, sales professionals create a natural momentum toward closing the deal.

Using Social Proof to Validate Credibility

One of the greatest barriers to decision-making in service sales is uncertainty. Buyers are often hesitant to commit due to fear of making the wrong choice, wasting resources, or facing internal resistance. Social proof, demonstrating that others have successfully navigated similar challenges, reduces the uncertainty and builds confidence in the decision.

In B2B sales, peer influence plays a significant role in shaping decisions. Research from Demand Gen Report shows that 97 percent of B2B buyers cite peer recommendations and case studies as the most reliable sources of information during the purchasing process. When evaluating new vendors, decision-makers want to see evidence that others in their industry have made similar choices and achieved positive outcomes.

A CIO considering a cybersecurity upgrade is more likely to move forward if they hear that other IT leaders in their industry successfully deployed the same solution with measurable improvements in security and compliance. A VP of operations evaluating automation tools will feel reassured knowing that peer companies have reduced downtime and increased productivity after implementation. The most effective sales professionals embed these success stories naturally into their conversations, making social proof an integral part of the decision-making process.

Instead of saying, "Our solution has helped many companies improve efficiency," a more compelling approach is to state, "One of our clients in the manufacturing sector reduced production errors by 40 percent within the first six months of using this system. Would it be helpful to discuss how they achieved that?" This approach not only provides credibility but also invites the customer to visualize the potential impact on their own business.

Structuring Conversations for Maximum Impact

Strategic conversations should follow a clear structure that moves the discussion forward while keeping the customer engaged. A proven framework for service sales conversations involves four key stages: discovery, alignment, validation, and commitment.

A conversation might start with discovery, where the sales professional asks open-ended questions to understand the customer's pain points and business objectives. The discussion then moves into alignment, ensuring that the proposed solution directly addresses those challenges. Validation follows, using social proof, case studies, and data to reinforce credibility. Finally, commitment is secured by guiding the customer toward the next step in the engagement process.

A scripted example of this approach in action might look like this:

Sales Professional: "I understand that your biggest challenge right now is reducing operational inefficiencies. Can you share more about how that's impacting your team's ability to meet its goals?"

Customer: "We're seeing a lot of delays because our internal processes are outdated. It's causing frustration across multiple departments."

Sales Professional: "That makes sense. You're not alone. Many companies in your industry are facing similar issues. One of our clients, a logistics company, struggled with inefficiencies that led to shipment delays and customer dissatisfaction. After implementing a streamlined workflow automation system, they reduced delays by 35 percent in six months. Would it be valuable

The Room Goes Quiet

to explore how that might apply to your situation?"

Customer: "That would be helpful. We need to find a way to make our processes more efficient."

Sales Professional: "Great. Based on what we've discussed, it sounds like improving workflow automation is a top priority for your team. Would it make sense to set up a working session with your operations team to map out how this solution could be tailored to your needs?"

This structure ensures that conversations remain focused, meaningful, and actionable. By guiding customers through discovery, alignment, validation, and commitment, sales professionals increase the likelihood of a successful outcome.

The Power of Strategic Conversations in Service Sales

Strategic conversations drive decisions. They shape how customers perceive value, determine priorities, and assess risk. When service sales professionals master the ability to guide discussions with intent, they shift from being vendors to trusted advisors.

Integrating consistency and social proof into sales interactions ensures that every conversation builds momentum toward engagement. Customers who continuously affirm their priorities and see real-world evidence of success are far more likely to commit. By structuring discussions with a clear framework, sales professionals create an environment where decisions feel natural rather than forced.

The key to success lies in making conversations about the customer, not about the service. By understanding their world, reinforcing their own commitments, and validating their concerns with peer influence, sales professionals create long-term partnerships built on trust and measurable impact. The most effective sales leaders don't just sell, but they facilitate meaningful, strategic conversations that drive business transformation.

William Anderson

Case Study: From Bottleneck to Breakthrough

The Setup: A Small Engagement with a Much Bigger Opportunity

It started with a $50,000 roadmapping engagement, a focused, short-term effort to help a financial services company assess its cloud infrastructure and provide recommendations for streamlining operations.

The request came from Mark, a senior manager in platform operations. His team was responsible for maintaining and optimizing cloud infrastructure, ensuring that developers had a stable and efficient environment to deploy applications. Over the past year, they had been struggling with growing complexity, inconsistent deployments, and increasing delays in getting new applications into production.

Mark wasn't looking for a major overhaul. He just wanted an external perspective to validate what his team already suspected. Their platform had become too cumbersome, slowing down development rather than enabling it.

"We know we have inefficiencies," he said in our first call. "We just don't know the full scope of them yet. Leadership is pushing us to fix the bottlenecks, but before we make big changes, we need to know where to focus."

That was our opening.

Laying the Groundwork: Delivering Immediate Value

The engagement was scoped as a roadmapping and assessment session, working directly with Mark's team. Over two weeks, we analyzed their cloud infrastructure, deployment workflows, and operational inefficiencies.

The Room Goes Quiet

The assessment confirmed what Mark suspected: there were multiple manual processes slowing things down, inconsistent standards across teams, and a lack of automation in key areas. But it also revealed something he hadn't fully considered.

Their development and operations teams were spending nearly 40 percent of their time troubleshooting deployment failures. Infrastructure teams were caught in a cycle of reactive problem-solving, constantly firefighting instead of optimizing. Every attempt to scale was met with delays, inconsistencies, and risk.

In our final session, I asked Mark a simple question.

"If you could fix just one thing that would have the biggest impact, what would it be?"

He exhaled and leaned back in his chair.

"Honestly? If we could give developers a way to self-service deployments without getting operations involved every time, it would change everything."

That was the moment we knew there was a much larger opportunity ahead. But Mark's response was also a potential trap.

His enthusiastic "That's exactly what we need" could be misinterpreted as approval to move forward, when in reality, it was simply an acknowledgment of the problem.

So instead of assuming he was ready to sign off on the next step, I asked a clarifying question.

"That makes a lot of sense. How are you thinking about positioning this internally?"

Mark hesitated.

"I mean, it should be pretty straightforward," he said, but his voice had lost some of its certainty. "If I can show leadership how much time we'd save, I think they'll get on board."

This was the real signal. Mark understood what needed to change, but he hadn't yet thought through how to make the case to leadership. His pause told me he needed help framing the conversation in terms that decision-makers—not just technical teams—would understand.

Shifting the Conversation: From Execution to Strategy

Rather than jumping straight into proposing a larger engagement, we took a step back and focused on helping Mark shape a clear, compelling narrative.

"Let's map this out," I said. "What does leadership care about most when making these kinds of decisions?"

"Operational efficiency and cost savings," he said.

"Great. And how do they typically evaluate investments like this?"

"They want to see hard numbers: how much time we're saving, how it impacts delivery, and whether it justifies the spend."

Mark had all the right pieces, but he hadn't connected them yet.

"So if we frame this as an investment that directly speeds up software delivery, reduces operational overhead, and prevents engineering burnout, do you think that strengthens the case?"

"Yeah," he said, nodding. "That's exactly how I need to present it."

At this point, Mark didn't need to be convinced. He needed help in shaping the message.

The Room Goes Quiet

Expanding the Engagement: Guiding the Decision-Making Process

A few weeks later, we were invited to present our findings to Mark's boss, Tanya, the director of platform engineering.

Before we met with her, we did something critical. We asked Mark what Tanya's primary concerns were.

"Tanya doesn't care about the technical details," he explained. "She's looking at this from a strategic level. If this isn't solving a broader business challenge, she's not going to push for it."

That was the insight we needed.

She wasn't evaluating whether our approach was technically sound; she assumed it was. Her role was to determine whether this initiative was worth backing at the leadership level.

When she started asking questions, it confirmed our assumption.

"How does this impact developer velocity?"

"What would success look like six months from now?"

"What are the risks if we move too fast on this?"

She wasn't looking for technical validation. She was looking for a business justification.

She needed to understand not just what the technology did, but how it fit into the company's larger strategic priorities.

Instead of talking about infrastructure automation, we framed it as a strategic investment that would improve developer productivity and reduce operational overhead.

Instead of saying, "We'll improve deployment processes," we

positioned it as, "Your teams will deliver software faster, with fewer errors, and lower operational costs."

Tanya understood the potential, but she wasn't going to push for a full-scale implementation right away. She needed a clear, smaller success to point to before scaling across the company.

"This makes sense," she said. "But we need to see how it works on a smaller scale before committing to something bigger."

That was our opportunity to propose a pilot project. Not to prove the technology, but to show leadership that the process and outcomes could scale successfully across teams.

Scaling Up: From Pilot to Enterprise-Wide Strategy

Before launching the pilot, we set clear expectations.

- The goal wasn't just to show the technology worked because they already knew it would.
- The success criteria focused on adoption, efficiency improvements, and leadership buy-in.
- The key metric was whether this approach could be scaled successfully to other teams without significant additional complexity.

The results exceeded expectations:

- Deployment times dropped by 65%
- Developer productivity increased significantly, and teams no longer had to wait on infrastructure bottlenecks
- Operations, instead of being stuck in firefighting mode, became strategic enablers for innovation

Because expectations were set properly, leadership wasn't waiting to see if the pilot would fail. They were watching for signs that it was ready to expand.

The Room Goes Quiet

We had initially framed the pilot as a way to reduce developer bottlenecks for a single team, with an expectation that if they could see a 20–30 percent improvement in efficiency, it would justify scaling.

When the actual efficiency gains were more than double that, leadership immediately wanted to discuss next steps.

Within three months, we had expanded the scope from a $250,000 pilot to a multiyear roadmap for an enterprise-wide developer platform modernization initiative.

The conversation naturally evolved into a $5 million engagement to build a standardized, scalable developer experience across the company.

Lesson: Growth Comes from Partnership, Not Selling

Big deals don't always start big.

They start with a simple conversation about pain points. They start with understanding what success looks like for your customer, not what you want to sell.

By positioning ourselves as strategic partners rather than vendors, we didn't just sell them a solution. We helped them define their own transformation.

That's how a $50,000 assessment became a $5 million enterprise-wide modernization initiative.

William Anderson

Chapter 18: From Value to Commitment

Realization, Resistance, and Negotiation Under Pressure

Turning page after page of the proposal, the director of operations straightened in his chair, his expression tightening with concern. "I understand the solution," he said. "What I don't understand is why it costs three times more than doing this internally. Show me where the value is."

The sales team launched into their standard response: talking about best practices, accelerated timelines, and reduced risk. But the director wasn't having it.

"Stop," he said. "I don't need concepts. I need numbers. What's this worth in real dollars? If I put three million into this project, what do I get back? When? And how certain are you?"

The room fell silent. It was a moment that plays out daily in service sales: when good solutions fail because their value isn't translated into language decision-makers can act on.

Realization Before Agreement

A sales leader recalls the deal that changed how she thought about value. Her firm was pitching a major transformation program. The solution was solid. The approach was proven. But they were stuck.

Then she rebuilt the business case from the perspective of the operations and finance teams. Instead of leading with the transformation, she started with the cost of the status quo, the financial inefficiencies, and the operational bottlenecks. The pivot worked. The moment they showed how a 10 percent process improvement would free up $12 million in working capital, the deal moved forward.

The Room Goes Quiet

This is what realization looks like. Not when a buyer hears your pitch, but when they see the financial impact of staying where they are.

That's the turning point in services sales. Not when someone agrees your solution is good, but when they own the risk of not doing it.

The Stall Before the Yes
By the time a deal reaches negotiation, logic alone no longer moves the conversation forward. What blocks progress isn't usually price—it's doubt. Not about the offering, but about their own willingness to commit. To take ownership. To trust that what's being promised will actually deliver.

This hesitation isn't a setback. It's a signal. It tells you that the buyer is close to a meaningful decision. But too many sellers misread it.

Some push harder by adding more data, more justification, and more urgency. Others go silent or fold too early, offering discounts before the buyer ever asks.

The best sellers do neither. They hold space. They guide the conversation without chasing. And they understand the buyer isn't wrestling with the offer. They're wrestling with the consequences of saying yes.

A CIO sat across from a cybersecurity consultant. The solution was clear. The value was real. But the CIO focused on one line item: the price. The consultant didn't defend it. He asked one question: "What was the cost of your last breach?"

The answer reframed the entire conversation.

Anchoring in the Customer's Own Words
The most powerful moments in sales don't come from what you say. They come from what the customer says. When they articulate their own risks, your value becomes internalized. They're not being sold. They're defending their own decision.

It might sound like:

- "We can't afford another six months of these outages"
- "If we don't improve forecasting, we'll miss our margin targets again"
- "Our board won't accept another failed initiative this year"

When those words come from the customer, you're not convincing. You're confirming.

This is where questions become your most strategic tool:

- What's the cost of delay?
- How often do these issues resurface?
- What does this mean for your team's credibility if it fails again?

These aren't traps. They're invitations. And once the customer responds, silence is your ally.

The Power of Strategic Silence

Not every seller uses silence well.

A vice president of operations was reviewing a digital transformation proposal. After scanning the last slide, she said, "This is a significant investment. We need to think about it."

The room went quiet.

The sellers sat back in their chairs. One flipped a pen between his fingers. Another stared at the floor. Their eyes darted, but no one met hers. The silence felt empty, like the team had run out of answers.

The vice president closed her notebook and stood. "We'll be in touch."

The meeting ended there.

The Room Goes Quiet

That is the danger of silence without intent. When posture is slouched, energy flat, and presence absent, silence communicates hesitation, not confidence. Instead of giving the buyer space to wrestle with the decision, it signals the seller has nothing left to offer.

Later, we will look at a case study where silence was held with discipline. The posture was steady, eye contact calm, and the silence itself carried weight. That silence did not end the conversation. It created space for the buyer to name the risk of doing nothing, and that was the moment commitment took root.

From Realization to Resistance: Enter Procurement

And just when you think the deal is done, procurement walks in.

Skilled procurement professionals are trained to grind down deals. They bring price comparisons, alternate vendors, and sudden urgency. But their real motive isn't savings. It's risk transfer. They want cover. They want to be able to say: "We pushed hard. We got more."

You can't win that game by playing defense.

Procurement expects concessions. They expect sellers to blink. But services sales is different. You're not just offering a product. You're offering partnership, accountability, and outcomes. And that's where you hold your ground.

Trading Without Losing Trust or Control

When procurement says, "We need a 10 percent discount," don't just say no. And don't just say yes.

Say: "We can explore a rate adjustment if the contract extends to two years and you're open to a case study upon successful delivery."

This isn't semantics. It's strategy. You're not conceding, you're exchanging. You're making it clear that every give warrants a get. Because in high-stakes service sales, perception is reality.

William Anderson

And the moment you give something away without asking for anything in return, you lower the perceived value of what you offer. You reinforce the idea that your original price was inflated, your terms were flexible, and—worst of all—you can be pressured. That undermines confidence, even as you try to close the deal.

On the other hand, trading communicates conviction. It signals to procurement that you're not desperate; you're deliberate. That you know your value. And that you're willing to collaborate - on terms that respect both sides.

This is where many sellers stumble. They believe holding firm means refusing to move. But rigidity isn't strength. Thoughtful flexibility is. When you plan your trades, you stay in control. You remain adaptable without ever appearing weak.

Here's how it plays out in practice.

Scenario One: The Timeline Squeeze

Procurement says, "We need this project completed two months earlier."

The instinct might be to say yes to win the deal. But the better move is to link the acceleration to shared accountability.

You respond, "We can prioritize resources to accelerate delivery, but we'd need streamlined internal approvals and milestone payments in place to keep pace."

This does two things. First, it reframes the request as a joint effort, not a unilateral demand. Second, it preserves your margins and execution capacity while showing commitment to their timeline.

You didn't say no. You didn't roll over. You created alignment.

Scenario Two: The Support Add-On

They ask, "Can you include 24/7 support at no charge?"

The Room Goes Quiet

You counter, "That's typically a premium service, but I can include the first ninety days as part of our initial launch. After that, we can review usage and impact together."

You've just given them a win that feels significant but is limited in scope. It also opens the door to a future upsell, not a long-term drag on your delivery team.

Scenario Three: The Discount Push

They press for a price cut. You don't argue. You reframe.

"A discount reduces our ability to deliver results at full potential. But if a lower rate helps unlock internal approvals, let's look at options. A two-year commitment or case study agreement could make that viable."

This creates a trade: duration for discount, visibility for rate. And from their side, it looks like partnership, not pushback.

Why This Matters
In every trade, you're doing more than negotiating terms. You're shaping how the customer perceives you as a partner.

Give without asking, and you look like a vendor trying to close.

Trade with intent, and you become a partner driving outcomes.

It's the difference between being seen as a cost to be minimized versus a value creator to be invested in. But there's a nuance here, one that experienced sellers understand instinctively: never force the customer into a corner. The goal isn't to hold your ground at the expense of collaboration. It's to create clarity on shared value. A trade should feel mutual, not conditional. If it feels like an ultimatum, you've lost posture. But if it feels like alignment, you've built trust.

Customers respect when you ask for something in return. It tells them you're serious. It invites reciprocity. And it shifts the dynamic from a one-sided negotiation to a co-created partnership.

Let Them Feel the Win—On Your Terms

Procurement needs to walk away with a win. Your job is to let them, but without giving up what matters.

Offer high-perceived, low-cost items:

- A one-day training session
- Early access to new features
- Dedicated onboarding support for thirty days

Frame these as premium and offer them as the final give to close the deal.

You're not losing anything. You're locking in value, protecting margins, and closing with confidence.

A Composite Field Example

Let's bring this together with a composite field example.

A consulting team pitched a $4.8 million transformation project. The technical buyer was aligned. The executive sponsor was sold. The finance team pushed back hard: "This is 40 percent more than our internal estimate."

The seller responded by reorienting the conversation around the money story. They mapped out the operational inefficiencies: supply chain delays, duplicate systems, and customer churn. They quantified the current cost at $19.7 million per year and showed how a 15 percent improvement would deliver $7.5 million annually in retained margin.

That moved the deal forward.

At the decision point, hesitation crept in. "It's a big bet," the sponsor said. "What if it doesn't land?" The seller didn't defend the proposal. She asked, "What happens if you stay where you are?"

They sat in silence. Then the sponsor said, "We'll miss our year-end targets."

The Room Goes Quiet

The realization clicked. The resistance gave way to commitment.

Procurement entered with demands: price cuts, faster delivery, and extended warranty. The seller traded: extended support in exchange for case study rights, milestone payments for timeline acceleration, and a capped rate if renewal was automatic.

They walked away with a signed deal, full margin, and a customer ready to implement. Not because they conceded, but because they led with clarity, trusted the process, and negotiated with intent.

Commitment Over Agreement

The goal isn't just a signed contract. It's internal commitment.

When customers believe in the value, work through their hesitation, and defend the investment internally, you don't just win the deal. You set the stage for execution.

Realization drives momentum. Trust sustains it. Discipline at the end preserves it.

This is the arc of modern service sales, from value to commitment, through the gauntlet of resistance and negotiation.

In the next chapter, we'll shift from the art of closing to the science of scale. This is where the real test of services sales begins: delivering on what was promised.

Case Study: Ten Seconds of Silence

The Setup: A Decision Too Big for Logic Alone

Julien had delivered dozens of presentations, but this one mattered. The client was a manufacturing company under pressure from competitors, and their VP of Operations, Claire, had gathered her team to review the proposal.

The slides were crisp. The numbers made sense. Julien walked through operational bottlenecks, projected improvements, and the cost of delay. The business case was structured to speak to finance as much as to operations.

On the surface, everything lined up.

But Claire's body language told another story. She leaned back in her chair, arms crossed, and watched the final slide in silence. After a long pause, she spoke.

"This is a significant investment," she said. "We need to think about it."

Every seller knows the weight of that moment. Logic has been heard. The solution is understood. Yet the buyer hesitates. What blocks the deal is no longer facts, but the fear of committing to a decision they cannot walk back.

Holding Space When It Counts

Most sellers would have rushed in. They would have repeated another metric, defended the price, or offered a sweetener. Silence feels unbearable when the deal is on the line.

Julien did the opposite.

He lowered the remote onto the table. He steadied his posture and waited.

The Room Goes Quiet

Five seconds passed. Then ten. The room grew heavy with quiet. The operations leaders shifted in their seats, but Julien did not speak. He let the silence do its work.

Claire finally leaned forward. Her voice dropped lower, almost to herself.

"But if we don't act, we'll be outpaced in two years."

That was the moment. She was no longer processing Julien's argument. She was declaring her own. The realization was hers, not his. The commitment was internal, and it would last because she had voiced it herself.

Why Silence Works

Silence in that instant was not hesitation, it was presence. Julien had already made the case. By resisting the urge to fill the gap, he created the space for Claire to wrestle with her decision.

If he had spoken too soon, she might have nodded politely, thanked him for the presentation, and delayed the choice. Instead, she named the real risk out loud. Inaction was no longer safe.

When buyers hear themselves state the consequences of standing still, they stop being sold. They start defending their own decision.

The Outcome

Two weeks later, the contract was signed. No discounts. No extra concessions. The project launched with urgency because Claire owned the call. She did not just approve the spend. She championed it to her executive peers as her decision.

The momentum came not from Julien's last words, but from Claire's.

Key Takeaways: Commitment Is Earned in the Pause

William Anderson

- Silence is not absence. It is a signal of confidence that the case has already been made.
- Buyers need space to commit. If you rush to fill the gap, you rob them of the chance to own the decision.
- Realization creates commitment. When buyers voice the risk of inaction, the value becomes theirs to defend.

Deals are not won by the final sentence a seller delivers. They are won by the first sentence a buyer speaks after you stop talking.

Chapter 19: Selling the Long-Term Vision

Most sales professionals make the mistake of treating a closed deal as the finish line when, in reality, it's just the first step in a much longer journey. The true value of a customer isn't in a single transaction—it's in the lifetime of engagement that follows. The ability to expand that engagement is what separates short-term sellers from those who build lasting, high-value relationships.

Shifting from a 'project' to a 'partnership' mindset starts with how you position services from the beginning. Too often, sales teams present solutions in isolation by solving one pain point, addressing one challenge, and fulfilling one request. This approach limits the conversation to the immediate need rather than establishing a long-term vision. Instead, you should be positioning every deal as part of an ongoing value stream. Customers don't just need one-time solutions; they need a trusted partner who understands their evolving landscape and can guide them through continuous improvement, optimization, and expansion.

The First 90 Days Playbook: Using Early Success as a Springboard

The first ninety days after a contract is signed set the trajectory for the entire customer relationship. This period determines whether you become a strategic partner or just another vendor delivering a completed project. The companies that master expansion treat the first ninety days as an onboarding ramp for deeper engagement.

A structured playbook for the first ninety days includes three key elements:

- **Delivering Early Wins That Matter:** Customers don't just want results; they want proof that their decision was the right one. Prioritize high-impact deliverables that create immediate value and are visible to decision-makers. These quick wins should not only meet expectations but set the stage for bigger conversations.

- **Communicating Success to the Right Stakeholders:** Too often, the success of an engagement is confined to the team directly involved in the project. But expansions are approved by executives, procurement teams, and budget holders who may not be aware of what's been accomplished. Ensure that wins are socialized beyond the core project team through internal case studies, executive briefings, or progress reports that emphasize business impact.

- **Leading the Next Conversation Before the First One Ends:** Don't wait until the project is completed to discuss what's next. The most successful expansions happen organically because the groundwork was laid early. Every milestone should be framed as a stepping stone toward a larger goal. Use progress meetings to introduce ideas for optimization, efficiency gains, or strategic improvements that naturally require continued engagement.

Building an Expansion Narrative: Structuring Conversations That Lead to Bigger Deals

Expansion doesn't happen by accident. It happens because the conversations you have with customers make it inevitable. Instead of treating every project as a separate engagement, you should be guiding the customer through a journey where each phase builds on the last. This requires a well-structured expansion narrative that keeps customers looking ahead.

Every conversation should follow a natural progression:

- If you're discussing a solution for an immediate challenge, shift it toward what comes next once that problem is addressed
- If you're implementing a solution, discuss how to optimize it for maximum impact
- If you're optimizing, explore how to scale and extend

The Room Goes Quiet

those efficiencies across other areas of the business
- If you're scaling, introduce innovations and competitive advantages that can be achieved with deeper collaboration

Every conversation should feel like a beginning—not an end. Instead, each interaction should create momentum toward the next investment, the next opportunity, the next logical step in the partnership.

Proving Value Early to Secure Long-Term Success

A prime example of this approach in action comes from a service provider that turned a limited engagement into a $10 million long-term contract. It started with a small project focused on fixing a single operational issue. The team could have treated it as a one-and-done transaction, but instead, they executed a deliberate expansion strategy from the very beginning.

They made sure early wins were visible beyond the immediate stakeholders. They provided executives with insights into broader challenges they could help solve. Every milestone in the project wasn't just delivered. It was used as a springboard for bigger conversations.

By the time the initial engagement ended, the customer wasn't just satisfied; they were also seeing the provider as an essential partner in their long-term success. Expansion became the natural next step, and what began as a limited contract evolved into a multiyear, multimillion-dollar relationship.

The Key to Long-Term Customer Engagement

Selling the long-term vision isn't about *asking* for more business. It's about *leading* customers toward it. Customers invest when they see a clear path forward and trust that the risks are managed. The strongest sales professionals don't just close deals; they create opportunities that make future deals inevitable.

William Anderson

When you stop selling projects and start selling *partnerships*, you shift from being a vendor to becoming a long-term strategic asset. And in that shift, you unlock the kind of customer engagement that drives massive, sustained growth. Not every engagement builds naturally. Sometimes, what starts with momentum stalls quietly. And that's when the real skill of the service seller gets tested.

Chapter 20: Unsticking a Deal – Turning Stagnation into Momentum

In the world of services sales, momentum is everything. A deal that moves smoothly from discovery to close maintains urgency, engagement, and executive alignment. But what happens when that momentum stalls? When the once-eager buyer starts ghosting you, when emails go unanswered, and when procurement cycles stretch endlessly? The difference between a skilled salesperson and an average one is the ability to recognize red flags early and take decisive action to course-correct.

Recognizing the Warning Signs of a Stalled Deal

Deals don't stall overnight. It's a gradual process with warning signs that, if identified early, can be addressed before they turn into full-blown roadblocks. A deal might be in danger when meetings are repeatedly delayed, responses slow down, or your champion's language shifts from "when we move forward" to "if we move forward." Budget concerns can also emerge late in the cycle, often signaling a deeper hesitation from stakeholders. When procurement and legal teams drag their feet, it's usually because there's insufficient internal pressure to move forward. Perhaps most concerning is when executive attention shifts elsewhere, leaving your deal without a high-level advocate.

Spotting these signs early allows you to intervene before the deal slips into indefinite purgatory.

Reigniting Momentum with Strategic Interventions

Once a deal shows signs of stalling, taking swift action is essential. The longer it lingers, the less likely it is to close. The key to unsticking a deal is understanding why it has slowed down and addressing the root cause head-on.

Executive engagement is often the first place to look. If decision-makers have disengaged, reframe the conversation around strategic business impact. Remind them of the cost of inaction, whether that's lost revenue, competitive disadvantage, or operational inefficiency. Bringing an executive sponsor back into the loop can inject urgency and restore momentum.

If budget concerns have surfaced, shift the discussion from cost to value. Show how the service reduces the total cost of ownership, increases efficiency, or speeds up other key initiatives. When procurement becomes a bottleneck, work closely with your champion to ensure they are actively pushing internally. Providing pre-approved contract structures or introducing procurement-friendly financing options can help cut through bureaucracy.

When internal inertia is the issue, find new ways to engage the buying committee. Sometimes, introducing a fresh perspective—an industry expert, a reference customer, or an executive sponsor—can reinvigorate the discussion. Establishing internal milestones with the customer can also create natural deadlines that make progress feel necessary rather than optional.

Creating Urgency Without Artificial Deadlines

One of the worst mistakes salespeople make when trying to unstick a deal is relying on false urgency. Arbitrary end-of-quarter discounts or empty threats of price increases rarely work and can damage credibility. Instead, link urgency to meaningful business events. Fiscal planning cycles, regulatory shifts, or competitive threats provide natural motivators for action. Providing real-world examples of similar companies that acted and saw immediate impact can be a powerful way to reignite urgency.

Applying These Tactics to Services vs. Hybrid Deals

In pure services deals, the focus should be on impact, efficiency, and mitigating operational risks. Since services often require an ongoing commitment, aligning the engagement with broader strategic priorities is critical.

For hybrid deals that include services, hardware, and

The Room Goes Quiet

software, the emphasis should be on integration and de-risking implementation. Customers may hesitate because of uncertainty about how services will interact with existing technology. Proactively addressing concerns about complexity and transition planning helps eliminate these doubts.

Your Role in Moving the Deal Forward

When a deal slows down, it's easy to blame external factors: procurement, budgets, and internal politics. But the best sales professionals take full ownership of the outcome. If a deal is stuck, it's your job to unstick it. That means proactively diagnosing the issue, engaging the right stakeholders, and driving urgency through real business impact.

Sales isn't about waiting for customers to act. It's about guiding them toward confident decisions. Recognizing early warning signs, implementing the right interventions, and taking full responsibility for progress transform stalled opportunities into closed business. That's the difference between managing a pipeline and owning your success.

Chapter 21: Winning When You're Not There

Up to now, we've focused on the meetings you attend—the silences, the risks, the execution moments that decide whether you move forward or stall. But most deals don't die in those meetings. They die in the ones you'll never enter. The closed-door sessions. The budget debates. The executive reviews where your name is on the table but your voice is not in the room.

That's the blind spot in most sales books. They teach you how to run the meeting you're in, but they ignore the reality that the real decision happens later. The buyer who nodded with you now has to convince others. And that's where deals are lost— when your champion is left to carry the story unarmed.

The Champion's Burden

Every major deal depends on a champion inside the customer's walls. They are the one who believes in you enough to take a risk. But conviction isn't enough. Champions fail more often than they succeed, not because they lack influence but because they lack support.

They fail for three reasons:

- **Lack of story**: They can't explain the deal in a way that sticks
- **Lack of air cover**: They walk into tough rooms without reinforcement and get cut down
- **Lack of credibility**: They sound like they're repeating your pitch instead of speaking from their own conviction

If you don't equip them, you've asked them to fight an executive battle with bare hands.

The Room Goes Quiet

The Tools

Winning service sales is not only about the meeting you're in. It's about winning the meetings you'll never see. Your job is to arm your champion with tools that survive beyond you.

- **Executive Briefing Memo**: A one-page story in the customer's own language. Not a slide deck. Not jargon. A clear, concise brief that anyone in their organization can read, remember, and repeat. Without it, your champion is just a messenger, and messengers get shot
- **Fallback Plan**: Champions need cover when the hard questions land. "If they ask about risk, here's how to answer. If they press on cost, here's how to reframe it." You're not scripting them—you're preparing them. The fallback plan turns doubt into momentum
- **Decision Framework**: Map the options and outcomes in the language their decision-makers already use. If your story doesn't fit their framework, it won't survive the retelling. Deals die when the language doesn't travel

Two Champions, Two Outcomes

I watched a champion walk into the CFO's office armed with nothing but belief. They had conviction, but conviction wasn't enough. The CFO asked two pointed questions—one about risk, one about cost. The champion stumbled. The deal was dead in five minutes.

Months later, I saw the same seller support a different champion. This time the champion carried a one-page memo that laid out the upside, the risks, and the options. When challenged, they had prepared answers that shifted the conversation from doubt to confidence. The CFO didn't just hear a pitch; they heard conviction backed by clarity. Two weeks later, the deal was closed.

Same seller. Same solution. Different outcome. The difference was whether the champion was equipped to fight the internal battle.

What Carries Forward

You don't win because of what you say in the room. You win because of what carries forward when you're not there. The real test of execution is not how persuasive you sound in front of the buyer. It's how strong, clear, and credible your champion sounds in the rooms you'll never see.

That's the gap other books miss. They stop at the edge of the meeting. But the real work is making sure your story survives the retelling. If you want to win consistently, you have to learn to sell the meetings you'll never attend.

The Room Goes Quiet

Case Study: The Fortune 500 Procurement Trap

The Setup: When Price Becomes the Focus, You've Already Lost

We had spent months nurturing this account, carefully positioning ourselves as a strategic partner and building strong relationships with the internal teams. It was a textbook engagement, the kind where we had every reason to believe we were in control of the deal.

The customer was a Fortune 500 insurance company undergoing a major transformation. They were looking to modernize their IT operations, and our services were a critical part of their strategy. The vice president of infrastructure and operations, Michael, had been our internal champion from the beginning. He was responsible for leading the company's cloud transformation and had been pushing for this initiative for nearly a year.

Michael had brought us in early, ensuring we had direct access to his leadership team. Over several months, we worked closely with his senior director of cloud strategy and IT operations leadership, shaping the vision for their future-state architecture. The account executive, Sarah, had built a strong rapport with Michael, and the technical pre-sales consultant, Jason, had spent weeks crafting a tailored migration roadmap.

The opportunity was a multiyear services engagement worth over $5 million, spanning cloud strategy, implementation, and ongoing managed services.

By the time we reached the final stage of negotiations, everything seemed aligned. Michael and his team were enthusiastic. We had shaped the vision for what success looked like. The IT operations leaders saw us as a natural fit.

Then procurement got involved.

The Trap We Didn't See Coming

Procurement was introduced late in the cycle, right as we were expecting to finalize the contract. At first, their involvement seemed procedural—a matter of reviewing pricing and formalizing terms.

Then the emails started.

First, they asked for a pricing breakdown of our services. Then they wanted to benchmark our costs against alternative providers. Soon, they were pushing for aggressive discounts, citing comparisons with a smaller, lesser-known vendor who had underbid us by nearly 30 percent.

Sarah pushed back, reinforcing the business value we had established.

"Our approach isn't just about cost," she explained. "We've designed this engagement to align with your strategic goals. It's an investment in outcomes, not just a service contract."

Procurement wasn't interested.

"At the end of the day, leadership is asking for a cost-effective solution," the procurement lead replied. "If another provider can deliver at a lower price, we have to consider it."

We were no longer talking about business impact, risk mitigation, or long-term success. The conversation had been reduced to a numbers game, and we were playing on procurement's terms.

How We Lost Control of the Conversation

The moment procurement positioned us against a lower-cost competitor, the dynamic shifted.

The Room Goes Quiet

Instead of defending the value of our solution, we found ourselves defending our price. Every discussion revolved around justifying line items, proving cost efficiency, and countering the perception that we were overpriced.

At one point, Jason tried to reset the conversation.

"We're not just offering a service," he said. "We're bringing industry expertise, proven execution, and a track record of success with organizations at your scale. A lower price doesn't mean lower total cost of ownership. The real question is: will a 30 percent discount today cost you millions in inefficiencies later?"

Procurement wasn't moved.

"That's something leadership will have to decide," they said. "Right now, we need to get the pricing aligned."

Michael was caught in the middle. He still believed in the value of our approach, but as procurement took over negotiations, he had less influence over the final decision.

By the end of negotiations, we had dropped our pricing significantly, and not because we wanted to, but because we felt we had no choice. Procurement had reframed the entire engagement as a cost-reduction exercise, and in doing so, they had stripped away all the strategic value we had worked so hard to build.

We still won the deal, but it wasn't the win we wanted. Instead of a $5 million multiyear engagement, we signed a $2.8 million contract, heavily stripped down in scope.

Three months later, the customer ran into execution issues with the reduced scope of work, leading to cost overruns, inefficiencies, and delays in achieving their objectives.

We knew it was coming. But by the time they acknowledged the problem, it was too late. We were just another vendor, one that had conceded on price instead of standing firm on value.

How We Should Have Handled It

Looking back, our biggest mistake was letting procurement take control of the conversation.

We allowed the narrative to shift from strategic value to price competitiveness. And once that happened, we were on the defensive.

What we should have done:

- Set expectations early: Procurement's involvement wasn't a surprise. We should have anticipated their objections and prepared responses before they took control of the discussion.

- Kept Michael and his leadership team engaged: Once procurement became the focal point, we lost the support of our strongest allies. We should have kept IT operations leaders actively involved in defending the value of our services.

- Refused to engage in line-item negotiations: By breaking down our pricing, we gave procurement the ability to pick apart individual costs instead of evaluating the engagement as a whole.

- Introduced risk and outcome comparisons earlier: We should have forced the conversation to focus on why we were the best choice. Not just from a cost perspective, but in terms of business risk, execution certainty, and long-term outcomes.

Lesson: If You're Defending Price, You've Already Lost

After this experience, we changed the way we engaged with procurement-led negotiations.

We stopped treating procurement as a gatekeeper and started treating it as a stakeholder that needed to be managed from

The Room Goes Quiet

day one.

Every large deal from that point forward included:

- A clear procurement engagement strategy: We proactively framed procurement's role as a partner in ensuring business success, not just in negotiating price.
- A total cost of ownership analysis: Before procurement could position us as the expensive option, we presented a cost comparison that factored in risk, efficiency, and long-term business outcomes.
- A defined negotiation walk-away point: We established firm boundaries on what we would and wouldn't negotiate, ensuring that we protected the integrity of our service model.

A few months later, we were in another deal, this time with a global financial services company. Procurement once again tried to force a cost-cutting exercise.

But this time, when they asked for a line-item pricing breakdown, Sarah responded differently.

"We're happy to discuss pricing," she said. "But our proposal isn't a commodity bid—it's a business strategy. Before we discuss cost reductions, let's align on the risks associated with a lower-cost alternative. What's more important to your leadership team: short-term savings or long-term success?"

Procurement hesitated. Michael's counterpart in this company, the senior vice president of infrastructure, jumped in.

"We need success," he said. "I don't want to cut scope just to save money up front if it costs us more down the road."

That was all we needed.

William Anderson

Instead of caving on price, we refocused the conversation on outcomes. We won the deal without any price concessions.

Customers don't buy services. They buy outcomes.

The moment we allow procurement to dictate the conversation, we surrender control over the deal. But when we frame the discussion around business value, risk mitigation, and long-term success, procurement becomes just another stakeholder and not the final decision-maker.

This shift changed everything. It turned our sales process from a price-driven negotiation into a strategic value conversation. One where we set the terms, and where the lowest price was never the deciding factor.

Case Study: The $50,000 Discount That Should Never Have Happened

The Setup: A Small Concession That Got Out of Control

This deal had been progressing smoothly for months. The customer, a regional financial services company, was modernizing its loan processing platform to improve efficiency and reduce operational costs. Their existing system was slow, prone to outages, and increasingly expensive to maintain. The pressure was on. Competitors were already launching faster, more automated solutions, and their leadership team had made it clear that delays were not an option.

Our proposal was a comprehensive services engagement, designed to migrate their core application to a cloud-native platform, provide structured advisory support, and ensure a smooth transition with minimal disruption. The contract was scoped at $2.1 million. This was a fair price given the complexity of the migration, the ongoing training required, and the post-go-live support necessary to prevent rollout failures.

James, the senior director of IT architecture, was our champion. He had been pushing for this modernization for over a year, and he understood the risks. If this rollout went wrong, the entire lending division would feel it, not just IT.

But James wasn't the buyer.

He was responsible for making the technical case, but final approval had to go through procurement and finance, both of which we hadn't yet engaged.

As we were nearing final agreement, we weren't even negotiating with procurement yet. We were working with one of James's key influencers, the VP of IT operations, Matt.

"Look, this is all looking good," Matt said during one of our final internal discussions. "I think we can get this through, but it would really help if we could bring the number down just a bit. If you can take off $50,000, it'll make the internal discussions easier, and we can move forward faster."

Sarah, our account executive, saw no issue with this.

"I think we can make that happen," she said confidently. "We want to show we're flexible and invested in the partnership. I'll get that updated in the paperwork."

To her, this wasn't a loss—it was the way business was done.

"Sometimes you just have to give a little to get things closed," she told me afterward. "This will help us keep things moving. It's not a huge amount in the grand scheme of things."

I had my reservations. We hadn't even gotten to procurement yet, and we were already giving up margin. But Sarah had already set the expectation, and the deal was moving forward.

Then procurement got involved.

The Cost of Engaging in Pricing Before Reaching a Decision-Maker

When James took the proposal to procurement, we expected some pushback. What we didn't expect was how quickly they latched onto the fact that we had already moved on price.

"Appreciate you working with us on that initial adjustment," the procurement lead said in our first meeting. "Now let's talk about finalizing pricing. Leadership wants to see at least a 10% reduction before we can approve."

Sarah barely blinked.

The Room Goes Quiet

"We've already provided a $50,000 reduction," she countered. "That was done in good faith to help the internal discussions."

"Right, and we appreciate that," procurement replied. "But that wasn't with us. If there's already flexibility in pricing, we need to make sure we're getting the best deal for the business. Let's talk about what else we can adjust."

At this point, Sarah was on the defensive. Instead of reinforcing the value of our engagement, she was stuck justifying our pricing while facing increasing pressure to discount further.

"We like your proposal," the procurement lead continued, "but we have competing bids that are coming in lower. If we're going to move forward with you, we need another $100K off. Otherwise, leadership is going to push us toward one of the lower-cost options."

That should have been a red flag. Procurement was signaling that price, not value, was its primary focus. But because we had already given a discount before even reaching them, they saw pricing as flexible and expected more movement.

Sarah, feeling the deal slipping away, agreed.

"We want to be your partner," she said. "Let me talk with my leadership and see what we can do."

The next morning, she called me.

"They're not budging," she said. "We need to take the extra $100K off to close this."

We were now $150,000 below our original pricing, and procurement wasn't done yet.

The next email came in:

"One last thing. Finance is requesting that we extend the payment terms from Net 30 to Net 90. Let us know if you can accommodate that, and we should be good to go."

Then another:

"Also, leadership is questioning whether all the advisory hours are necessary. Can we trim some of that back?"

Then another:

"Given the cost adjustments, we're also looking at spreading implementation out over a longer timeline. Let us know if that's an issue."

By the time we signed the contract, we had lost $150,000 in discounts, were waiting three months longer for payment, had advisory services reduced by 40 percent, and had stretched the implementation timeline by an extra six months.

What We Should Have Done Differently

The mistake wasn't just agreeing to a discount. It was engaging in a pricing discussion before speaking with a final approver.

What we should have done:

- Set a firm pricing position before engaging with procurement: We should have reinforced our value and refused to discuss pricing adjustments until we were speaking with someone who had final decision-making power.
- Kept discussions with influencers focused on value, not price: We allowed Matt to push us into a discount before we were at the negotiation table. We should have kept the conversation around business impact and let procurement drive the pricing discussions.
- Refused to engage in line-item discounting: Once we started reducing scope and price in pieces, procurement kept finding more places to chip away.

The Room Goes Quiet

Lesson: Price Discussions Should Only Happen with a Decision-Maker

From that point forward, every deal included:

- A firm pricing model with a clear walk-away point
- A strategy for influencer-level discount requests, ensuring we only discussed pricing with individuals who had signing authority
- A structured way to frame discounts, ensuring any price adjustments were tied to specific scope changes, not just arbitrary cuts

Months later, we found ourselves in a similar negotiation.

When procurement asked for a 10 percent discount, Sarah responded differently.

"Our pricing is structured based on the outcomes we're delivering. If we remove budget, we have to adjust scope. What's more important to leadership: keeping the full scope or lowering cost and adjusting the timeline?"

Procurement backed off. We closed at full value.

Customers don't buy services. They buy outcomes.

And when we don't defend the investment required to deliver those outcomes, we're not just

William Anderson

Case Study: The Multimillion-Dollar Deal Saved by a Strategic Risk Discussion

The Setup: When Value Isn't Enough Without Risk Ownership

I knew the moment Andrei, the CFO, leaned back in his chair that we were at the tipping point.

For the past hour, the meeting had gone exactly as planned. The technical deep dive had been smooth. The financial model was defensible. The implementation timeline was aggressive but achievable. The team had handled every question with precision, checking every box. But the moment I saw the shift in Andrei's posture—his fingers lightly tapping against the table, his expression neutral but unreadable—I knew.

He was hesitating.

Not because the numbers didn't work. Not because he didn't see the value. But because something deeper was holding him back.

I had seen this before.

Years earlier, in a different boardroom, I watched a team lose a deal we should have won. Back then, we had done everything right on paper. We had the best proposal, the strongest references, and the most polished delivery. But when the CFO voiced concerns about risk, we tried to sell harder. We reassured, redirected, and doubled down on the positives. Within forty-five minutes, the deal was gone.

That was the day I learned a hard truth. When a leader hesitates, it is not because they need more reasons to say yes. It is

The Room Goes Quiet

because they do not yet trust that saying yes will not come back to bite them. The worst mistake you can make in that moment is pretending risk does not exist.

I was not going to make that mistake again.

The Turning Point: Naming the Risk

Andrei finally spoke. His voice was steady, but the weight behind it was clear.

"I just don't see how this doesn't become another budgetary nightmare," he said. "We've been burned before. What makes you different?"

He wasn't asking about features. He wasn't questioning our capabilities. He was looking for a reason to walk away.

I saw my colleague inhale, ready to respond, and I knew exactly what he was about to say: something about our experience, our track record, and our process. The exact kind of answer that had cost us that last deal. I cut in before he could speak.

"You're absolutely right to be concerned."

Andrei's eyes flicked to me, just for a second. He had not expected agreement. He had expected a defense. A pitch.

Not this time.

I let my words settle before continuing.

"If I were in your position, I'd be asking the same question. How do we know this won't fail? Let's not avoid the conversation. Let's get ahead of it."

I clicked the remote, and the screen changed.

William Anderson

A single slide. No flashy graphics. No charts. Just one title:

Three Ways This Could Fail—And How We'll Handle It.

The tension in the room shifted. A few people leaned forward slightly. Andrei's fingers stopped tapping. This was different.

Too often, sales conversations treat risk like a dirty word, something to be minimized, danced around, or covered with enthusiasm. I had watched a team lose a deal because of that exact mistake. This time, I was bringing risk to the forefront.

Owning the Failure Modes

I let the first scenario sit on the screen before speaking.

"Let's start with the most common failure point: scope creep."

One of the project managers exhaled, just barely audible. I knew he had lived with this pain before.

"We've seen it happen. What starts as a fifteen-million-dollar project turns into twenty million, then twenty-five. Suddenly leadership is forced to explain what went wrong. Our approach is simple. We cap and phase. We set hard checkpoints where we reassess, and any expansion must be justified by measurable ROI before a single dollar is added."

No one interrupted.

I moved to the next point.

"Second: internal resistance. The biggest threat to a successful implementation is not the technology. It is people. Resistance from key teams can kill even the best projects."

Across the table, the head of operations shifted slightly in her chair. She had seen initiatives die at the hands of internal politics

The Room Goes Quiet

before.

"That is why we integrate a full adoption framework, mapping out stakeholder engagement in advance. And if resistance flares up, we already have a playbook for that."

I clicked again.

"Third: vendor accountability. You've probably been in this situation before. Six months in, your vendor is pointing fingers, your team is frustrated, and the project stalls."

Andrei's reaction was immediate. A small shake of the head, just short of a scoff. He had been in that situation before.

"That is why we contractually embed accountability checkpoints. If we miss, we pay. If we fall behind, we correct before you feel it."

And then I stopped talking.

I did not try to fill the silence. I let the weight of the conversation settle.

The Moment the Deal Turned

Andrei picked up the printed version of the deck and flipped through it. He wasn't looking at the case studies anymore. He wasn't scanning the ROI slides. He was reading the section on risk. Processing.

Finally, he nodded.

"I appreciate that," he said, tapping his fingers against the table once more. "It's the first time someone has walked in here and told me exactly how this could fail instead of pretending it won't."

That was it. That was the moment I knew we had won.

Two days later, the contract was signed: fifteen million dollars, locked in.

Lesson: Risks Don't Kill Deals—Ignoring Them Does

Executives are not afraid of making a bad decision. They are afraid of making an unprotected one—the kind that, if it goes wrong, leaves them holding the blame, the consequences, and the fallout.

That hesitation—the crossed arms, the silence, the skeptical look—is not a request for more reasons to say yes. It is a signal that they do not yet trust that saying yes will not come back to haunt them.

Too many teams fail in that moment because they assume more enthusiasm will get the deal across the line. They try to redirect, reassure, and emphasize past successes. That is when the deal starts slipping away.

We lost that deal years ago because we thought the CFO needed more proof that our solution would succeed. But what he really needed was confidence that if something went wrong, we would not leave him holding the bag.

This time, we gave him exactly that:

- Instead of avoiding the risk conversation, we brought it to the forefront.
- Instead of pretending failure was not a possibility, we showed we had already mapped out how to handle it.
- Instead of expecting him to take the risk alone, we demonstrated that we were taking it on with him.

The Room Goes Quiet

That is what closed the deal.

If you are in a deal that seems like it should be moving forward but keeps stalling, stop selling and start securing. Look for the unspoken hesitation. Read the signals. And when you find them, do not ignore them. Own them.

Because the difference between a lost deal and a signed contract is not who has the best offering. It is who has the best answer to the most important unasked question:

What happens if this goes wrong?

William Anderson

Chapter 22: Mastering Procurement – Winning Against Cost-Centric Buyers

"We love your solution, but procurement has the final say."

If you've ever heard this, you know exactly what comes next. The deal slows down, the conversation shifts from value to price, and suddenly, you're being pressured to lower costs just to keep the opportunity alive.

Procurement is not your customer. They exist to minimize spending, extract the most concessions, and keep you away from the executives who actually see the impact of your solution. Their playbook is built around leverage, and if you don't recognize their tactics early, you'll find yourself negotiating against yourself.

Too many service sellers assume that procurement is just a formality. It's not. Procurement shapes the final terms of the deal, and if you don't take control, they will. The key to winning is shifting the conversation away from cost-cutting and positioning your service as the only logical choice.

Understanding Procurement's Playbook

Imagine you've spent months working with a senior executive. They're excited, they see the value, and they tell you they want to move forward. Then, procurement steps in, and suddenly everything changes. The urgency disappears, and the negotiation resets.

Procurement follows a predictable playbook designed to weaken your position and make it harder for you to push back. They will tell you that your service is similar to others in the market, even if it's not. They will claim that budget is locked, even when it isn't. They will manufacture urgency, insisting they need your best offer by the end of the week, only to delay the decision

The Room Goes Quiet

again. And they will hint that a competitor has come in lower, hoping you'll panic and match a price that may not even exist.

The most effective tactic they use is isolation. They tell you they'll relay information to the executive team, cutting you off from the actual decision-makers. The moment they succeed, you lose your ability to reinforce value, reframe the discussion, or prevent the deal from becoming a pure price negotiation.

Shifting the Conversation from Cost to Value

Procurement wants to make price the focal point of the conversation. If you accept that framing, you're already at a disadvantage. Instead, the discussion needs to center on the total cost of ownership, risk mitigation, and long-term impact.

A company once had two options for a service provider. One was significantly cheaper, but their implementation track record was weak. The other provider was slightly more expensive but had a guaranteed time-to-value. Procurement, focused purely on cost, chose the cheaper option. Six months later, the project was scrapped due to integration failures, costing the company five times the original savings.

This happens more often than companies want to admit. Procurement rarely accounts for the long-term consequences of its choices. That's why it's your job to make sure they do.

- **Tie cost savings to business outcomes, not discounts:** Instead of lowering price, highlight the financial impact of your service. A discount saves them money once; an operational improvement saves them money every quarter. If you can quantify efficiency gains, reduced downtime, or risk avoidance, cost-cutting arguments lose strength.

- **Expose the risks of going with a cheaper alternative:** Ask how they are factoring in vendor stability, execution risk, and long-term service quality. If they aren't, walk them through what happens if an underbidding competitor fails to deliver.

- Connect your value to executive priorities: Procurement cares about cost. Leadership cares about business impact. If you can align your value proposition with the CEO's or CFO's goals, procurement will have a much harder time making this about price alone.

If procurement is focused on minimizing cost, your goal is to expand its definition of cost to include everything beyond the price tag.

Breaking Procurement's Gatekeeping Role

One of procurement's favorite tactics is keeping you away from the people who actually want and need your service. If you allow them to control access to decision-makers, they will filter every conversation through a cost-cutting lens. You need to re-engage the economic buyer without making procurement feel like you're going around them.

There are subtle but effective ways to do this. If procurement is stalling, you can create urgency by positioning executive alignment as a natural next step. If the delay is artificial, framing your engagement as a strategic priority can bring leadership back into the discussion. And if you have a strong champion within the business, you can use their voice to reinforce the importance of moving forward.

A simple way to break procurement's control is by mirroring their own tactics. If they create urgency, you can too. If they insist on process, you can insist on aligning with key stakeholders. The key is to be assertive without being confrontational. Instead of asking permission, state why executive engagement is necessary.

"We want to make sure this aligns with the broader business strategy before finalizing details. Can we set up a quick review with [Executive Name] to confirm priorities?"

This keeps the conversation open-ended while signaling that procurement isn't the only authority in the decision.

The Room Goes Quiet

Avoiding Procurement's Negotiation Traps

Many service sellers walk straight into procurement's most common traps. Knowing how to recognize them can prevent unnecessary concessions and keep the deal from spiraling into a price war.

- The "best and final" bluff: Procurement will often ask for a final offer, implying that if you don't lower your price now, the deal is dead. In reality, this is usually just a pressure tactic. Instead of reacting, hold firm and reinforce that final pricing should be discussed with the full decision-making team.

- The fake competitor play: Procurement will claim that another provider came in 15 percent lower. Sometimes this is true, but often, they're testing how flexible you are on pricing. The best response is not to panic but to ask what differences exist between the proposals. If they can't provide details, you know they're fishing.

- The never-ending approval cycle: You finalize pricing, but then legal needs to review. Then finance. Then security. Each step drags out the process, and each delay is an opportunity for procurement to push for additional concessions. The best way to counter this is to force a clear path to close. Ask them who else needs to sign off and what the timeline is.

- The take-it-or-leave-it ultimatum: Procurement may say they have a fixed budget and can't go beyond a certain amount. This is rarely true. Budgets shift for strategic priorities. If they push this narrative, suggest involving leadership to reassess the investment. This puts pressure back on procurement rather than on you.

Winning Against Procurement

The biggest mistake service sellers make is treating procurement as if it were the final decision-maker. It isn't. Procurement exists to push for cost savings, but leadership makes the ultimate call on strategic initiatives.

- Own the narrative by keeping the conversation focused on business impact rather than price
- Re-engage executives early and often to prevent procurement from controlling the discussion
- Refuse to chase bad deals by walking away if procurement is only focused on price and refuses to acknowledge value
- Expose hidden costs by making them justify the risks of a low-cost provider
- Control the timeline to prevent unnecessary delays and additional concessions

Procurement only has as much power as you give it. If you let it dictate the terms, it will always push for lower pricing. If you redefine the conversation, make value the center of the discussion, and re-engage decision-makers, procurement's leverage disappears.

The only way to win against procurement is to make its cost-cutting agenda irrelevant.

Chapter 23: Scaling Execution into Repeatable Success

Execution earns trust. But scale sustains it.

The most disciplined service sellers don't just close deals. They build motion. They apply what works and strip away what doesn't. They create repeatability not just in delivery, but in how they engage, qualify, position, and close. What starts as intuition becomes architecture.

Take Ace, a service manager at a global enterprise software company. Before adopting the frameworks in this section, his pipeline was populated with inconsistent opportunities: some small, some strategic, most stalling before commitment. But after applying collaborative qualification, value framing, and risk-based positioning, his motion changed. In just two quarters, both the number and average size of qualified deals in his pipeline more than doubled. These approaches weren't the only driver, but they were a significant influence—giving him a structured, repeatable method to scale the kind of deals that mattered.

That's what scaling execution looks like. Not just more effort. Better motion.

You've seen how trust is built through execution:

- Qualification becomes collaborative
- Value is constructed, not just pitched
- Risk is surfaced and owned
- Conversations turn into commitments without chasing

Now it's time to make that motion predictable. To move from high-performer behavior to high-performance systems. Because your next level of growth doesn't come from grinding harder. It comes from scaling what already works.

William Anderson

Part IV: Scale—Building Sustainable Success

The Room Goes Quiet

Chapter 24: Scaling Service Sales Without Losing Strategic Value

The Challenge of Growth Without Dilution

The leadership team at a fast-growing technology consulting firm sat around a conference table, reviewing the numbers. Demand was higher than ever, but operational inefficiencies were slowing them down. Each engagement was treated as a one-off, requiring extensive customization, long sales cycles, and unpredictable delivery timelines. Scaling seemed like an impossible task without sacrificing the high-touch, strategic value that had made them successful in the first place.

"We can't keep doing this," the COO admitted, rubbing his temple. "Every deal is starting from scratch, and our teams are drowning in bespoke projects. We need a way to scale without becoming just another transactional service provider."

The solution didn't lie in automation alone, nor in forcing a rigid, one-size-fits-all structure. It required a fundamental shift: balancing repeatability with customization, ensuring that efficiency didn't come at the expense of strategic value.

Building a Scalable Sales Approach Without Losing Customization

For years, service sales had been dominated by the idea that the more customized the engagement, the more valuable it was to the customer. But as organizations tried to scale, this approach became unsustainable. Instead of starting from scratch every time, the most successful firms embraced modular service design—a framework that allowed them to maintain flexibility while dramatically improving efficiency.

One professional services firm struggling with growth found success by breaking its offerings into three core categories:

assessment and strategy, implementation, and ongoing support. Each category contained predefined service components that could be combined based on customer needs. Sales teams no longer needed to create new proposals from the ground up. Instead, they used structured modules to build tailored solutions quickly, reducing complexity without sacrificing adaptability.

This approach changed everything. Sales cycles shortened. Delivery teams had greater clarity on scope and execution. Customers appreciated the transparency and predictability. Most importantly, the firm retained its strategic advisory role while significantly increasing deal velocity.

Field Note: Repeatability Revealed Their Strategic Value

At a growing enterprise software firm, a regional services leader named Jay found himself fielding constant complaints from customers, sales, and delivery. Every deal felt like a one-off. Services weren't scoped consistently. Sales would promise custom outcomes, and delivery would scramble to reverse-engineer a plan on the fly. No one knew what "good" looked like, and every engagement started from zero.

Jay led a pivot.

He worked with a small team to dissect their most successful projects, breaking them down into modular phases: discovery, implementation, and optimization. They built playbooks, standardized core deliverables, and created messaging that helped sales sell outcomes, not hours. Within one quarter, not only were deals closing faster, but delivery was reporting smoother handoffs, and customers were clearer on what to expect.

The real win? Their largest renewal that quarter came with a simple note from the customer: "This felt different. It felt like you'd done this before."

Repeatability didn't dilute their strategic value. It revealed it.

The Room Goes Quiet
Ensuring Consistency Without Stifling Sales Agility

As the technology firm continued its transformation, another challenge emerged: maintaining consistency across sales and delivery teams. Too often, sales professionals positioned services in ways that delivery teams couldn't realistically execute, leading to misaligned expectations and frustrated customers.

A senior sales director recognized the issue and proposed a radical shift. Instead of letting each salesperson define engagements in their own way, the company developed a structured sales playbook, a guiding document that outlined service tiers, pricing strategies, customer success benchmarks, and expansion pathways.

The playbook didn't eliminate flexibility, and it provided a shared framework. Sales professionals could still tailor conversations to customer needs, but within clearly defined parameters that ensured deliverability. When a new client engaged, both sales and delivery teams spoke the same language, reinforcing trust and improving execution.

With this structured yet adaptable approach, deals progressed more smoothly. Customers knew what to expect, sales teams operated with greater confidence, and delivery teams had a clear roadmap for execution.

Scaling Without Losing the Customer Experience

One of the biggest fears in scaling service sales is losing the high-touch engagement that differentiates strategic providers from commodity vendors. The IT consulting firm knew that increasing deal volume couldn't come at the cost of customer relationships.

Instead of allowing post-sale engagement to become an afterthought, they embedded it directly into their operating model. Every new client was introduced to a customer success roadmap, a structured plan that ensured they saw long-term value beyond the initial sale.

From the start, the company scheduled onboarding sessions to align expectations, quarterly business reviews to track measurable outcomes, and executive strategy discussions to explore long-term growth opportunities. These touchpoints weren't just about retention; they reinforced the company's role as an ongoing partner in the client's success.

As a result, renewal rates skyrocketed. Customers no longer viewed the firm as a service provider but as an indispensable part of their business strategy.

The Leadership Shift That Drives Sustainable Growth

Scaling service sales is not just a process challenge—it's a leadership challenge. Organizations that attempt to scale without strong leadership often find themselves growing revenue at the expense of strategic value.

One company struggling with stagnating service sales saw a transformation when a new sales director stepped in with a different philosophy. Rather than focusing purely on quarterly targets, he instilled a culture where customer impact was the primary measure of success. Every major deal required a post-sale success plan, ensuring customers weren't just sold a service but received measurable business outcomes.

This shift had a ripple effect. Sales teams stopped viewing deals as one-time transactions. Delivery teams became more invested in ensuring long-term results. Customer advocacy increased, leading to organic growth through referrals and expanded partnerships.

Breaking Down Silos Between Sales and Delivery

Many service providers struggle with an invisible but destructive barrier: the disconnect between sales and delivery teams. Sales teams often overpromise, setting unrealistic expectations, while delivery teams are left scrambling to execute under tight constraints. This misalignment leads to frustrated customers,

The Room Goes Quiet

burned-out employees, and damaged reputations.

A consulting firm facing this exact challenge introduced a co-ownership model, where account executives and delivery leads shared responsibility for customer success. Sales teams were no longer incentivized just to close deals but also accountable for ensuring those deals resulted in satisfied, long-term clients.

With this new model, project completion rates improved, misaligned expectations decreased, and customer satisfaction scores rose. By integrating sales and delivery teams into a shared mission, the company turned its biggest internal challenge into a competitive advantage.

Sustaining Growth by Building a Culture of Ownership

Scaling service sales isn't just about refining operations. It's about fostering a culture where teams take ownership of customer success beyond the sale. Organizations that create this culture don't just grow revenue; they build deep, lasting relationships that fuel long-term sustainability.

A global consulting firm once struggled with high employee turnover. Many sales professionals saw their roles as transactional, focused solely on deal closures rather than long-term impact. Leadership recognized that to truly scale, they needed a cultural shift.

They launched internal leadership programs that emphasized mentorship, strategic thinking, and customer advocacy. Instead of rewarding employees purely on short-term sales metrics, they incentivized post-sale engagement and customer expansion. Over two years, both employee retention and customer satisfaction saw dramatic improvements.

When leaders actively participate in post-sale engagement, champion customer success initiatives, and create pathways for professional growth, they lay the foundation for sustained performance.

Scaling Service Sales Without Losing Strategic Value

The firms that successfully scale service sales without becoming commoditized are those that:

- Balance efficiency with flexibility, ensuring repeatability without sacrificing customization
- Align sales and delivery teams under a shared framework to improve execution and customer trust
- Embed long-term customer engagement into their process, reinforcing value beyond the initial sale
- Foster leadership that prioritizes customer success, cross-team collaboration, and ongoing strategic value

Service sales is evolving, and organizations that scale with a structured yet adaptable approach will be the ones that thrive. Growth should never come at the expense of strategic value. When done right, scaling strengthens customer relationships rather than diluting them.

The Next Evolution of Service Sales: Intelligence, Automation, and AI

Once an organization successfully scales service sales, the next challenge is staying ahead of market shifts.

In today's business environment, AI, automation, and platform-based ecosystems are reshaping how customers engage with service providers. Buying cycles are evolving, stakeholder influence is shifting, and the expectation of real-time, data-driven decision-making is higher than ever.

The next section is not about AI replacing service sales professionals. It's about how AI is reshaping the battlefield—providing insights, automating administrative friction, and enabling sales teams to predict customer needs before they even surface.

The Room Goes Quiet

Those who master AI-driven decision-making will accelerate revenue, shorten sales cycles, and improve customer alignment. Those who ignore it will find themselves losing deals not to better competitors, but to customers who believe they can do it themselves.

The most scalable service firms aren't those who reduce complexity at the cost of customer impact; they're the ones who turn complexity into clarity. They don't just scale processes—they scale strategic intent. When every customer engagement follows a framework grounded in measurable outcomes, strategic value isn't diluted. It has become the standard.

William Anderson

Case Study: The "Just Do It Internally" Deal Saved by Mentor-Based Approach

The Setup: When "We'll Do It Internally" Isn't the End of the Conversation

The meeting had all the signs of a deal slipping away. The conversation was professional and polite, but too polite. The discussion moved smoothly, but there was no urgency, no real engagement beyond surface-level agreement. Underneath it all, there was an unspoken resistance.

At the center of it was Meera, the senior director of IT operations. She had the calm confidence of a leader who had seen vendors come and go, who had built her career on delivering results *without* relying on outside help. She wasn't dismissive, but she was firm.

She leaned back slightly in her chair, exhaled, and spoke with a steady voice. "This has been great, and I appreciate all the work your team put into this. But we're going to handle this in-house. We have the expertise, and it makes more sense for us to execute internally rather than bringing in outside services."

The words settled in the room. It was the kind of moment where a less-experienced sales team might have pushed harder or backed off entirely. Both mistakes would have cost them the deal.

Daniel, the lead seller, did neither. He didn't argue. He didn't launch into another pitch. Instead, he nodded slightly, leaning back just enough to match Meera's posture.

"That makes a lot of sense," he said. "Walk me through how you're thinking about execution."

The Room Goes Quiet

A pause. Meera glanced at Priya, her lead architect, before responding. "We'll have our internal engineering team own the rollout. They'll stand up the automation framework, integrate it with our existing infrastructure, and optimize the workflows as we go."

Daniel turned to Priya. "That's a big lift. Do you feel good about the scope and timeline?"

Priya hesitated. Just for a second.

"We do," she said carefully. "There's going to be some ramp-up, but we've handled similar projects before."

That hesitation was small—but meaningful.

Meera quickly stepped in to reinforce the decision. "We're confident in our team's ability. We just need to stay disciplined on execution."

Daniel nodded again, still measured. "Of course. And if things start to slip, what's your contingency plan?"

For the first time, the room went quiet.

Meera exhaled slowly. Priya looked down at her notes. The VP of operations, who had been quiet until now, finally leaned forward. "We haven't defined one yet."

It was a small crack, but it was there.

Daniel let the silence do the work before speaking. "I get it. You've got a strong team, and the last thing you want is to bring in outside help that takes away ownership. I've seen this a lot in companies like yours, where highly capable teams choose to run projects internally to maintain control. But I've also seen how execution can get stretched."

Meera didn't argue. She didn't need to. They both knew it was true.

Daniel continued, adjusting his tone slightly, making it less about pitching, more about *coaching*.

"But let's not frame this as a binary 'internal versus external' choice. What if instead of hiring us to 'do the work,' you had us as a backstop? What if your team led execution, but we acted as a mentor-based consulting partner by giving you best practices, troubleshooting issues as they arise, and helping you avoid the mistakes we've already seen play out elsewhere?"

Meera lifted an eyebrow, just slightly. "Go on."

"Your team drives this. They stay in full control. But we provide the strategic guidance, proven frameworks, and troubleshooting when you need it. Not as a replacement for your expertise, but as a way to accelerate your success."

Priya sat up a little. "So we'd still own the work, but you'd act as a safeguard?"

Daniel nodded. "Exactly. Think of it like an experienced mentor standing behind your team. You don't need us every day, but when you hit something unexpected, we make sure it doesn't slow you down. Instead of spending weeks figuring out something, you get immediate answers. Instead of trial and error, you start with best practices."

Meera exchanged a look with Priya. Then she turned back to Daniel. "Alright," she said. "Let's explore what that would look like."

The Result: How Mentor-Based Consulting Became the Backstop They Needed

What started as a firm decision to handle everything internally became a strategic engagement that allowed Meera's team to move faster without giving up control, resulting in the following:

The Room Goes Quiet

- Reduced implementation time by 40% by avoiding common pitfalls that would have otherwise caused delays
- Maintained full ownership while gaining a structured support system that enabled more confident execution
- Prevented costly delays by having immediate access to expertise when problems arose, eliminating weeks of troubleshooting

Three months into the engagement, the difference was undeniable. Meera's team wasn't just keeping pace—they were ahead of schedule. Instead of feeling like they had lost control by involving an external partner, they realized they had gained control by having a trusted backstop.

By month six, they expanded the engagement. What began as an occasional troubleshooting resource became a trusted advisor role, with the team proactively leaning on external expertise to guide long-term strategy.

Key Observations: How to Identify and Shift the Buyer's Mindset

Red flags to watch for:

- Framing the decision as 'internal vs. external': If a leader views the choice as binary, they are more focused on control than value.
- Overconfidence in execution without a clear contingency plan: If they can't clearly outline what happens if things go off track, the risk is underestimated.
- Small moments of hesitation from the team: Even a brief pause or glance between colleagues can signal doubts that haven't been fully discussed.

How to Shift the Buyer's Mindset:

- Reframe the conversation: It's not about hiring services. It's about providing a safety net that ensures success.
- Position external support as a mentor, not a takeover: If a team feels like they are handing over ownership, they shut down. If they see an experienced partner standing behind them as a safeguard, they lean in.
- Let them feel the weight of their own uncertainty: Instead of telling them where their plan is weak, ask the right questions and let them come to the realization themselves.

Lesson: Why 'We'll Just Do It Internally' Is Rarely the End of the Conversation

When a buyer says, "We're handling this in-house," it's not a rejection—it's a defense mechanism. It's a way to maintain internal credibility, control, and budget.

But more often than not, they aren't rejecting expertise. They're rejecting the idea that they have to *give up control* to get it.

The key isn't in convincing them otherwise. It's giving them a better way to win.

The mentor-based consulting approach worked because it didn't challenge Meera's expertise or authority. It simply gave her team an experienced backstop to turn to when execution got complicated. Once she saw that external expertise wasn't a threat but a competitive advantage, the conversation shifted.

She didn't buy because she was sold. She bought because the right path became undeniable.

The Room Goes Quiet

Chapter 25: From Sales to Execution – Building Trust at Every Step

The most dangerous moment in any sales process isn't the close—it's the handoff. This is the moment when excitement meets execution and where vision turns into delivery. And it's also where deals often begin to unravel. When the handoff is poorly managed, what was promised and what's delivered no longer match. Customers feel misled. Delivery teams scramble. Margins erode. And worst of all, trust evaporates.

This isn't just a process flaw. It's a credibility crisis.

Why Handoffs Fail

The root of the issue is organizational distance. Sales and delivery often operate on different planes. One side is incentivized to close. The other is measured on execution. Sales paints the vision, tells the story, and secures the commitment. Delivery lives in timelines, resource constraints, and execution realities.

When those two worlds fail to intersect early, the result is chaos. Customers are caught in the middle. They believed one version of the story and were delivered another. The perception becomes one of bait-and-switch, even when it wasn't intentional.

And customers don't blame internal misalignment. They blame broken promises.

From Function Handoff to Team Integration

Organizations that get this right don't just improve a step in the process. They erase the line between sales and delivery. Instead of a handoff, there's continuity. The people selling the solution are connected to those delivering it from the start. It's not about delivery owning the sale. It's about delivery having visibility and a voice in what's being promised.

This doesn't just prevent scope issues. It builds trust internally and externally. Sales becomes more informed. Delivery is better prepared. The customer gets one consistent narrative.

That consistency is the foundation of trust.

Digitize the Experience, Not the Relationship

This alignment isn't just about function—it's also about format. In a world transformed by remote work and digital-first selling, how customers experience your service has shifted. But what hasn't changed is their need for relationships, consistency, and trust.

Remote selling taught organizations how to scale. But in 2024 and 2025, the pendulum is swinging back toward hybrid models. In-person meetings are resurging. The lesson isn't to abandon virtual but to integrate both.

Remote engagement offers efficiency and reach. In-person interactions create depth and influence. A sustainable, high-trust sales approach blends both with intention.

Hybrid Engagement that Builds Alignment

The best service sellers adapt fluidly between virtual and in-person. Early-stage discovery and qualification are often faster and more scalable over video. But key milestones: executive alignment, final negotiations, and post-sale success reviews should be considered moments of human connection.

Bringing delivery teams into those engagements, especially at transition points, builds shared ownership. It also demonstrates to the customer that your company isn't structured in silos. Everyone's pulling in the same direction.

That's a signal of reliability. And reliability is the soil where trust grows.

The Room Goes Quiet

Accountability Models that Prevent Misalignment

Misalignment isn't always malicious. Often, it's just unaccountable. Sales is rewarded for signing the deal. Delivery is measured by executing it. No one owns the gray space in between.

Fixing this doesn't mean blaming teams. It means designing systems that align incentives and outcomes.

Sales leaders should remain engaged past the close. Not to micromanage delivery, but to ensure promises are kept and expectations remain intact. Shared metrics across teams, like time to execution readiness, margin retention, and post-handoff satisfaction, tie the success of the sale to the success of the outcome.

When both teams rise and fall together, alignment becomes habit.

Avoiding the Bait-and-Switch Trap

There is no faster way to destroy trust than to deliver something that doesn't match what was sold. And in service sales, those mismatches are often subtle—differences in scope interpretation, timelines, assumptions.

To eliminate this, you need one shared truth.

Sales decks, contracts, statements of work, and delivery plans should mirror the same commitments, expectations, and outcomes. If a customer compared the marketing message to the implementation plan, there should be no daylight between them.

And where ambiguity exists, resolve it early. Vague promises are the enemy of execution.

William Anderson
The Trust-Accelerating Power of In-Person Moments

There are moments when trust accelerates more quickly in person than over video, such as during executive meetings, critical negotiations, and quarterly business reviews. In these moments, presence carries weight. It signals importance, respect, and commitment.

Even casual in-person meetings, like coffee catchups or shared meals, carry strategic value. Behavioral science backs this. People who eat together negotiate better, cooperate more, and walk away with stronger relationships.

This isn't about formality. It's about proximity. Shared space breeds shared understanding.

Make the Virtual Feel Personal

Still, most interactions in a scalable model happen virtually. That means sellers and delivery leaders must be fluent in building trust through screens.

Start with small but human touches. Send personalized intro videos instead of generic emails. Use a virtual "coffee on us" card before a call. Bring unique insights into the conversation that show you've done your homework.

On video calls, always turn your camera on. Look at the lens, not your screen. Be animated, structured, and concise. Use collaborative tools like MURAL, a visual platform used for mapping and brainstorming ideas, to make remote conversations more interactive and memorable.

It's not about replacing in-person meetings but making virtual feel personal.

The Room Goes Quiet

Measuring the Invisible

What gets measured gets managed. And trust—while hard to define—is reflected in measurable outcomes.

Track post-handoff satisfaction. Monitor scope adherence. Watch for margin erosion. Measure how often sales stays engaged after the deal. Look at renewal rates and expansion growth.

These are the signals of aligned execution and maintained trust.

When misalignment exists, the numbers will show it long before the customer walks away.

A Success Story of Integration

A mid-sized technology firm faced rising churn. Sales was high-performing. Delivery was overworked. Customers were frustrated. The gap? No real integration between the teams.

To fix it, they removed the "handoff" altogether. Sales and delivery were brought together in cross-functional pods. Deals couldn't close until delivery signed off. Sales stayed involved post-sale. Four metrics were tracked obsessively: customer satisfaction, scope fidelity, margin retention, and readiness speed.

The result? Renewals went up. Delivery stress went down. And sales didn't slow. They accelerated.

Because trust compounds. And trust starts when teams act as one.

The Bottom Line

There is no handoff. Not really. There's only a customer journey that starts with a promise and ends with an outcome. Anything less than total alignment along that path breaks trust.

William Anderson

Service sales isn't about selling a solution. It's about selling a result. And results are only real when delivery can bring them to life.

The future belongs to service organizations that eliminate the friction between selling and executing. They build hybrid engagement models with human depth. They replace vague commitments with clear agreements. They make virtual interactions personal and in-person meetings strategic. And treat the relationship—not the process—as the product.

Sell the result. Deliver the promise. And make every step of the journey feel like one seamless experience.

That's how trust scales.

The Room Goes Quiet

Case Study: Breaking the Growth Ceiling

The Breaking Point

The services team at a rapidly growing medical device company had a problem most teams would envy—demand was surging.

Every customer wanted high-touch onboarding, access to senior consultants, and ongoing support. And for a while, they delivered. But by the time they crossed one hundred enterprise customers, the cracks were visible. Backlogs were growing. Service timelines were slipping. And the internal team was stretched so thin that even the most seasoned consultants, like Carlos, were working late nights to keep projects afloat.

Failure to evolve wasn't just inconvenient but existential. Customers were beginning to question response times, and competitors were offering simpler onboarding models. Internally, implementation leaders such as Isabella were signaling burnout. Leadership, led by Karen, the VP of Services, knew something had to change. But how?

The Risk of One Size Fits All

The team realized the problem wasn't demand but delivery design. Every new customer was treated like the first. Each engagement was tailored, every timeline negotiated, and every resource stretched to meet inconsistent expectations. Sales, under David, promised "whatever it takes." Delivery scrambled to keep up.

It worked until it didn't.

What they needed wasn't more effort. It was structure.

Reframing the Services Strategy

Rather than trimming services or raising prices, Karen and her leadership team redefined how services were packaged and delivered.

They analyzed eighteen months of delivery data and identified patterns. Most customers followed one of three paths: rapid onboarding with limited touchpoints, guided implementation with coaching, or high-complexity deployment involving stakeholder engagement and long-term planning.

They launched a new model with three clearly defined tiers:

- **Foundational**: Streamlined onboarding with core configuration and minimal support (ideal for hospitals adopting standard workflows)
- **Guided**: Hands-on implementation with access to consultants, training modules, and post-go-live advisory
- **Strategic**: End-to-end partnership model for complex hospital systems with multiple stakeholder groups, integrations, and scaling roadmaps

The tiers weren't just scoped. They were branded, priced, and aligned with buyer personas across hospital systems.

The Sales Shift

David brought his sales teams in early. Instead of selling effort, they began selling outcomes. Instead of negotiating implementation steps, they offered choices based on value and strategic fit.

Sales teams, now armed with clear value propositions for each tier, were more confident in positioning services during early conversations. They shifted from reactive to proactive expansion selling. The upsell conversation became natural. Procurement discussions were faster. And for the first time, delivery could plan ahead.

The Room Goes Quiet

From Trust to Growth

Customers responded. Mid-size hospitals that once asked for enterprise customization were happy with the guided package when it was clearly framed. Large health systems appreciated the transparency and chose higher tiers based on outcome alignment, not cost alone.

Internally, delivery satisfaction improved, burnout dropped, and implementation speed increased. The team didn't just improve operational efficiency. They re-established trust.

By the end of the fiscal year, the company saw:

- 17% increase in services margin
- 2x increase in customer renewals tied to implementation success
- 50% faster time-to-value on strategic accounts

Impact Snapshot: What Changed When Services Were Tiered Intentionally

Before: Every deal was bespoke. Scope was reactive. Delivery was overwhelmed.

After: Sales led with outcomes. Services were scoped to fit. Delivery ran on confidence, not chaos.

Result: Customers still felt heard. But now, they also felt a sense of consistency and clarity.

The real breakthrough wasn't just in the structure but in the clarity it created across teams. With this model in place, sales, delivery, and customer success could now operate from the same playbook and unlock repeatable, scalable growth.

William Anderson

Chapter 26: When the Room Stays Quiet: Resilience and Identity as a Service Seller

Take a breath. Step out of the stories for a moment. This chapter isn't about what happened in someone else's deal—it's about you. Where you're headed. Who you're becoming. Because sooner or later, you'll sit in a room that stays quiet. You'll do the work, carry the risk, and leave with nothing to show for it. A deal will stall, a quarter will miss, a door will shut. It will feel like the silence swallowed you whole. And in that moment, the question isn't whether you can sell. It's whether you can keep going.

This is where the real shift happens. You're not just a seller chasing wins. You're a professional risk-carrier. An execution partner. Someone whose identity is built on consistency, credibility, and resilience—not on a single deal's outcome.

Most people reading books like this will nod along at the tactics and maybe use them once or twice. Fewer will make the shift I'm talking about here. But if you do—if you see yourself as the person who absorbs the toll and keeps standing—then you'll create impact. That impact will help define your career, affect those you work with, and shape success for your customers.

The Toll of Carrying Risk

Carrying risk is not about surviving one tense meeting or one tough quarter. It is the accumulation that wears you down. Every silence, every rejection, every deal that slips past quarter-end adds weight. Over time, that weight shifts from the deal to you. You start measuring your worth not by who you are, but by what closed—or didn't.

That is the real danger. The toll is not financial. It is personal. If you don't have a way to absorb it, you begin to see yourself as fragile or replaceable. The work hardens some sellers into

The Room Goes Quiet

cynics. It breaks others entirely. The best use the toll as proof of endurance. They turn it into credibility, because buyers trust the person who has been tested and still shows up sharp.

The Identity Shift

"I'm a salesperson" is too fragile an identity. It cracks with every loss. If you want to last, you need a stronger frame. You're not a quota-carrier. You're a risk-carrier. An execution partner. A professional who stands in high-stakes rooms, names the risk, and shoulders it alongside the buyer.

That identity doesn't collapse when a deal falls through, because your value is not tied to one transaction. It is defined by the way you show up, deal after deal, year after year.

Resilience Practices

Resilience is not a mindset slogan. It is a discipline. These practices keep you sharp when the weight threatens to grind you down:

- Recovering from silence that doesn't break: When a room stays quiet and the deal dies, don't rewrite the story as a personal failure. Capture what happened, learn what you can, and move forward. Silence is data, not a verdict on who you are
- Debriefing a lost deal without losing confidence: Treat every loss as a postmortem. Which pillar cracked? Where did you fail to equip your champion? Write it down. Own it. Then stop. You lost a deal, not your ability
- Building credibility through consistency: Buyers don't believe in you because you never lose. They believe in you because you keep showing up with discipline, clarity, and integrity. Wins create momentum. Consistency creates reputation

The Deal That Almost Broke Him

I knew a seller who lost a career-defining deal. The kind of loss that feels like a verdict. For weeks he carried it like a scarlet letter. But he didn't quit. He dissected the failure, owned what was his, and kept showing up. A year later he won a deal twice as big—the one that defined his career. The resilience didn't erase the loss. It turned it into the proving ground that made the win possible.

The Call That Went Wrong

I was in a high-stakes negotiation with a senior executive. The pressure was obvious before anyone spoke. The executive had not prepared. They had not reviewed the material, and their lack of readiness exposed them in front of their own team.

I executed as expected. I pressed, I held the line, and I backed the executive into a corner. My internal team applauded me afterward. Senior leaders told me I had "held the customer's feet to the fire" and "not played their games." All of that was true. But as soon as the call ended, I knew something was wrong.

The executive had only two paths. They could accept the loss of face, bring us in anyway, and hope their performance was forgotten. Or they could throw us under the bus, blame everything on us, and kill the program to save themselves. By the next morning, I had my answer. The call came: we were accused of not playing in good faith, and the deal was dead.

I stayed resilient and prepared for the worst. I looked hard at what we could have done better, how the four pillars applied, and what it would take if the deal came back to life. I armed my team with the insights I had drawn so we would be ready if the chance came. A week later, the deal was back on the table. We moved forward, and the executive got to present it as if they had saved the day.

Resilience didn't just keep me standing. It gave me the perspective to recover, adjust, and let the customer save face—even when the cost was high in the moment.
What Lasts

This is not about closing one deal. It is about becoming the kind of person buyers believe in year after year. Service sales is not

The Room Goes Quiet

a sprint. It is a career measured by how you carry risk, recover from loss, and return with your discipline intact.

The room will go quiet many times. Sometimes it will break your way. Sometimes it will not. Resilience is what ensures you are still standing for the next one—and ready when the deal that defines you finally arrives.

Chapter 27: Preparing for the Future of Service Sales

The service sellers who win in the next five years won't be the ones with the most technical knowledge, the most pre-built content, or the longest resumes.

They'll be the ones who can scale trust without scaling risk.

That means more than just tightening handoffs or packaging smarter offerings. It means rethinking what customers expect when they buy services and how we show up to deliver that value at every stage of the journey.

Because the future of service sales isn't linear. It's not about moving faster through a fixed set of steps. It's about building systems that adapt, people who align, and conversations that stay grounded in outcomes, even when everything around them changes.

The leaders who embrace this won't need to chase product features or one-time wins. They'll own the momentum. They'll set the tone for how their organizations qualify, position, deliver, and grow. And they'll do it with repeatability—not just intuition.

Imagine this:

A customer enters a QBR already knowing the outcomes they received last quarter. Not because someone told them, but because the system showed them. The AE speaks to pipeline and growth. The services lead speaks to operational efficiency and business impact. The customer isn't asking, "What's next?" They're asking, "How do we do more of this?"

That's not a fantasy. That's where this is headed.

The Room Goes Quiet

But only if we lead it there.

If there's one constant throughout this book, it's this:

Success in service sales is no longer a result of individual heroics. It's the product of alignment: between strategy and execution, between customers and internal teams, and between trust and results.

You've now seen how strategic empathy, disciplined execution, and systemized delivery form the foundation of high-performing services organizations.

The next step is codifying that foundation, so it scales without you.

Because you shouldn't have to carry every deal on your back.

In the next section, we pull together the full system: maturity models, frameworks, and transformation levers that help you build a repeatable services-led go-to-market motion. One that doesn't just win deals—but earns the right to grow them.

Chapter 28: Adapting the Framework for Scalable, Sustainable Service Sales

The first time the new sales framework was rolled out, it failed.

Not because it lacked logic. Not because it wasn't tested. It failed because it was delivered from the top down, packaged in new terminology, accompanied by polished decks, and launched with high expectations but no ownership.

The team listened. Nodded. Took notes. But within two weeks, old habits returned. Conversations defaulted to product. Discovery was rushed. Trust fell flat. The framework didn't fail on paper. It failed in practice—because it didn't feel like theirs.

This is where many organizations stumble. They treat transformation like software: plug it in, flip the switch, and expect compliance. But sales don't change because of a framework. Sales change when a new approach makes sellers more effective, more confident, and more valuable in the eyes of the customer.

This chapter is not about elegance. It's about what works.

It offers two vantage points: one for the individual practitioner looking to transform how they sell, and one for the business leader responsible for making that transformation scalable and sustainable. Both are essential. Both must begin where most change fails: at the point where theory meets resistance.

The Practitioner's Path: Turning Insight into Action

You're in the room with a customer. The dialogue is good. There's interest. Engagement. Forward motion. Then the tone shifts.

"We'll take this back and evaluate our options."

The Room Goes Quiet

You nod. They smile. Everyone shakes hands. But something's off. The conversation didn't collapse, but it didn't convert either.

This wasn't about pricing. It wasn't about competition. You lost control of the moment that mattered most.

The best sellers don't let that moment drift. They own it.

They don't wait for objections—they surface them. They don't pitch—they frame. They don't sell certainty—they become the person who *brings* it into the room.

A great seller might pause, then say:

"I understand this is a serious commitment. What I've seen in similar projects is that the real risk usually isn't the technology but the transition. If this drags on another six months, what does that mean for your Q4 targets?"

That's not pressure. That's perspective.

It reframes the conversation around stakes, not specs. And it's the difference between being a vendor with a product and a partner with a plan.

This framework isn't about rehearsed lines or clever counters. It's about operational leadership within the sales process, guiding customers through uncertainty, and helping them move with conviction.

To make that real, start here:

- Lead discovery with risk, not capability: Uncover what's at stake before you talk about what's possible. Identify what your buyer loses if nothing changes.
- Use customer language to define impact: Echo the terms they use internally for financial targets, operational inefficiencies, reputational risk. Make

the case in *their* metrics, not yours.

- Frame post-sale success from the first meeting: Speak to the outcomes on the other side of delivery. Let them feel that you're already invested in what happens after the contract is signed.

You don't need permission to sell this way. You need clarity, courage, and a commitment to execution. When practiced consistently, these shifts build longer relationships, unlock larger opportunities, and reposition you as the person they call when the stakes rise.

The Leader's Path: Scaling What Actually Works

You're reviewing quarterly performance. The pipeline looks healthy, but it's not converting. Pricing pressure is creeping up. Margins are tightening. And it's not just external competition. It's internal inconsistency.

Some sellers are thriving. Others are stuck. The variance isn't talent. It's clarity.

You don't need more activity. You need a system that enables more effective action.

But system change in service sales is high risk. Done poorly, it creates friction between teams, confuses messaging, and fragments execution. What you need isn't a playbook for sellers but a framework for the business. One that turns services from cost centers into strategic assets.

Here's how that starts:

1. Align the Leadership Team Around the Why

Before training anyone, align the people responsible for leading the change. Hold a working session with senior sales, delivery, and finance leaders. Together define:

The Room Goes Quiet

- What's broken in the current model
- Where sales stalls or falls short
- How the new approach reframes value through the lens of trust, risk, and customer outcomes

When leaders align on philosophy, frontline teams get clear on what matters.

2. Pilot, Don't Preach

Don't start with a global rollout. Select a group of adaptable, insight-driven sellers and arm them with the new model. Track outcomes:

- Deal cycle velocity
- Number of stakeholders engaged
- Renewal and expansion patterns

Use this pilot to gather proof points, tune the message, and build internal champions before scaling.

3. Build a Structured but Adaptable Engagement Model

Leave less to chance. Codify:

- When risk conversations enter the process
- How qualification assesses customer maturity
- What strategic assets (case studies, executive briefs, and account plans) are used at each stage

Structure creates consistency. Flexibility enables ownership.

4. Shift the Metrics to Match the Model

If you keep measuring booked revenue alone, the team will game the system for short-term wins. Redefine what good looks like:

- Multiyear deal growth
- Contribution margin and delivery fit
- Net revenue retention (NRR) over initial contract size

Incentivize outcomes, not activity. Align rewards to sustainable growth.

5. Vet Your Advisors Against the Right Standard

If you bring in external support, whether consultants, trainers, or enablement partners, ask hard questions:

- Do they treat services differently from product sales?
- Can they facilitate real conversations about risk and ownership?
- Do they prioritize lifetime value over initial win rates?

If the answer is no, you're buying a playbook for the wrong game.

Culture Change at the Point of Sale

Service sales performance doesn't improve because people learn new terminology. It improves when those terms reflect how customers *actually* buy. The real test of any framework is simple: does it help a customer move forward when the decision is hard?

Because that's where service sales lives: in complexity, in doubt, and in moments where trust matters more than price.

The teams that win don't outsell by volume. They outsell by conviction. They listen with precision, speak with clarity, and act with ownership.

The Room Goes Quiet

And their sellers don't wait to be told what to do. They internalize the framework. They shape it to fit their accounts. They lead.

From Framework to Differentiation

This isn't a silver bullet. It's not designed to be easy. But it *is* designed to work because it reflects the real behaviors of top performers and the real conditions customers face.

When you lead with risk, anchor in outcomes, and own the post-sale journey, you stop being one of many. You become the one they trust.

The framework is here. The tools are in your hands. The next move is yours.

Let it be a move that sticks.

William Anderson

Part V: The Future of Service Sales— Adapting to a Changing Landscape

Chapter 29: The Future of Service Sales

The Evolution of Service Sales in an AI-Driven World

Service sales has always been about solving problems. The best sales professionals don't just close deals. They guide customers through uncertainty, help them mitigate risk, and unlock new opportunities. But as artificial intelligence, automation, and digital transformation accelerate, the very nature of service sales is shifting. AI isn't replacing sales professionals; it's making them sharper, more insightful, and more indispensable than ever before.

For decades, selling services relied on relationships, expertise, and a deep understanding of industry trends. These qualities still matter. But now, AI allows sales teams to see patterns that were once invisible, anticipate customer needs before they arise, and personalize solutions at a level no human could manage alone. The old model—where a salesperson relied on intuition and experience to identify potential clients—has been replaced by AI-driven systems that analyze thousands of data points in seconds.

At a global IT consulting firm, the head of sales used to spend hours manually reviewing reports to determine which industries were most likely to invest in digital transformation. Now, an AI-powered system does it in moments, identifying not only high-potential sectors but also individual companies within them, flagging key decision-makers and even suggesting the best time to engage. The firm's sales teams no longer waste time chasing the wrong opportunities. Instead, they focus on the conversations that matter, the ones where they can truly make an impact.

AI and Automation: The Engine of Scalable, Intelligent Sales

AI is already changing how service providers engage with customers, qualify opportunities, and structure their offerings.

Instead of blindly pursuing leads, AI-driven CRM systems analyze historical data, buying patterns, and behavioral signals to determine which prospects are most likely to convert. Instead of relying on sales scripts that apply to everyone, AI-driven recommendation engines help craft hyper-personalized proposals based on industry trends, customer needs, and market conditions.

At a cybersecurity firm, the sales team no longer relies on generic outreach emails. Every engagement is now shaped by real-time AI insights. Before calling a prospect, a sales rep already knows what security challenges their company has faced, what compliance risks they're concerned about, and how they stack up against competitors in their industry. They don't waste time with a canned pitch. They start the conversation with insight and with solutions tailored before a single word is spoken.

Meanwhile, automation is eliminating the administrative friction that once slowed service sales to a crawl. Intelligent assistants now schedule follow-ups, generate customized proposals, and handle contract management with precision, allowing sales teams to focus on high-value interactions. A consulting firm that once took three weeks to generate a detailed service proposal now does it in under an hour.

This is not about replacing sales professionals. It is about freeing them to do what they do best: build relationships, drive strategic conversations, and create long-term value.

From Transactional Selling to Platform Thinking
Service sales is no longer about winning one deal at a time. The shift toward platform-based business models is reshaping how companies engage with customers, moving from one-time engagements to long-term, continuously evolving relationships.

Companies like AWS, Microsoft Azure, and Google Cloud have set the new standard. They don't sell cloud infrastructure in isolation, but they provide platforms that integrate seamlessly into their customers' businesses, adding value long after the

The Room Goes Quiet

initial sale. Their approach isn't about pitching a service once. It's about embedding themselves so deeply into their customers' ecosystems that switching providers becomes unthinkable.

That same shift is now playing out across industries. Healthcare providers are no longer selling isolated AI-powered diagnostic tools; they are building continuous data-driven ecosystems that adapt to evolving patient needs. Manufacturing firms are not just offering automation consulting but are delivering smart factory platforms that optimize supply chains in real time.

For service sales professionals, this changes everything. Selling is no longer about closing a deal and moving on. It is about positioning a service provider as an indispensable, ongoing partner.

A senior sales executive at a global software company put it bluntly during a recent strategy meeting: "We don't sell projects anymore. We sell evolution. Customers don't just buy a solution from us. They buy continuous improvement."

The Rise of Developers and Software in Sales Strategy
Another fundamental shift is the growing role of software and developers in corporate decision-making.

In the past, sales engagements were driven primarily by business leaders, procurement teams, and finance departments. Today, technical stakeholders—developers, engineers, and data scientists—are playing an increasingly central role in how companies select and integrate new services.

A financial services firm exploring fraud detection solutions no longer goes through the same months-long procurement process it once did. Instead, its development team integrates an AI-driven fraud detection API into its system in a matter of days, testing it before making a larger investment. If the technology proves valuable, scaling happens instantly.

This shift is forcing service sales teams to rethink their approach. Traditional sales pitches are no longer enough. The future belongs to companies that provide self-service access to their solutions, allowing developers to experiment, integrate, and extend services on their own terms.

A VP of sales at a leading AI company recently admitted, "Our biggest competitor isn't another vendor but the customer's own engineering team. If we don't make our solutions developer-friendly, we lose."

Service sales teams now need to engage with both business leaders and technical buyers. They need to understand how software ecosystems operate, how APIs drive adoption, and how to position services as long-term strategic enablers, not just point solutions.

AI is Not the Enemy—It's the Ultimate Sales Enablement Tool
There has been endless speculation about whether AI will replace sales professionals. The truth is the opposite. AI is not eliminating sales, but it is making it more precise, efficient, and scalable.

Imagine a sales professional with an AI-powered assistant that analyzes customer sentiment, market conditions, and past engagement history to craft the perfect outreach message. Instead of guessing when to follow up, AI predicts the optimal timing for engagement. Instead of manually tracking a customer's product usage, AI alerts the sales team when a client is likely to need an upgrade, weeks before they request it.

This is not the future. It is already happening.

AI is not making salespeople obsolete. It is amplifying their capabilities, allowing them to focus on creativity, relationship-building, and strategic problem-solving rather than getting bogged down in routine tasks. The best sales teams of the next decade will not be the ones that replace human insight with AI,

The Room Goes Quiet

but the ones that seamlessly integrate the two.

Leading the Next Era of Service Sales

The companies that will dominate the future of service sales are the ones that embrace AI, automation, and platform-based business models. They will shift from transactional sales cycles to embedded, evolving partnerships. They will recognize that software, developers, and APIs are just as critical to adoption as executive buy-in. They will see AI not as a threat, but as a tool that enhances their ability to deliver value at scale.

Sales is no longer about persuasion. It is about alignment. Customers don't want to be convinced to buy something. They want to work with partners who understand their challenges, anticipate their needs, and evolve alongside them.

The future of service sales belongs to those who adapt, who embrace AI as a force multiplier, and who understand that the true measure of success isn't closing a deal but creating a relationship that grows over time. Those who recognize this shift will lead the next generation of sales. Those who don't will be left behind, not by AI, but by competitors who know how to use it to win.

William Anderson

Chapter 30: The Limits of AI in Service Sales – Where Humans Still Win

By 2025, AI will have reshaped the way sales teams operate, bringing unprecedented efficiency, automation, and insight. It can analyze vast amounts of data, predict deal outcomes, and streamline outreach, but here's the reality: AI doesn't close deals. People do. AI doesn't build trust. AI doesn't navigate the messy, human complexity of corporate decision-making. AI can tell you which deals look promising, but it won't be the one sitting across from a skeptical executive, reading the room, adapting the conversation, and turning hesitation into confidence.

That's because service sales isn't just about logic and data. It's about relationships, influence, and strategic execution. AI is a force multiplier for good sellers, but it will never create great ones. The best sales professionals will use AI as a tool, not a crutch—leveraging its capabilities while recognizing its limits.

AI's Capabilities vs. Human Strengths

What AI Does Well	Where Humans Win
Automates lead scoring and outreach	Builds deep personal trust with buyers
Predicts deal success based on data	Reads emotional and political nuances
Surfaces relevant case studies instantly	Frames messaging based on buyer motivation
Generaters proposals and pricing quickly	Negotiates in complex multistakeholder environments
Identifies risk signals in patterns	Adapts instinctively to unique deal environments

AI operates in absolutes. It works in patterns and probabilities. It recognizes trends and surfaces insights at a speed no

The Room Goes Quiet

human can match. But selling is rarely absolute. It's situational, dynamic, and deeply personal. Successful sales professionals don't just react to data but interpret nuance, manage emotions, and adjust their approach in real time.

The problem isn't what AI can do, but what it can't. AI can generate a perfect email sequence, but it won't recognize when a buyer is hesitating for reasons that have nothing to do with the solution. It can suggest an optimal price based on historical deals, but it won't know when a customer is willing to pay more in exchange for a strategic concession. AI moves deals forward, but humans close them.

Where AI Falls Short in Service Sales

Selling at the highest level is about more than just following a process. It's about knowing when to challenge, when to wait, and when to push forward. It's about reading the room and anticipating objections before they're spoken. AI, for all its power, isn't built for that kind of dynamic engagement.

AI struggles with emotional intelligence. It can analyze sentiment in an email, but it doesn't understand what's left unsaid. Buyers often mask their true concerns behind corporate language, and only an experienced seller can extract the real objections. A prospect might say, "This looks promising," and AI will mark it as a positive signal. But a human sales professional picks up on the hesitation, the half-second pause, the subtle tension in their voice, and recognizes that "promising" is just a placeholder for doubt.

It also fails at navigating corporate politics. Enterprise deals are never just about one person's decision. They involve layers of influence, competing priorities, and power struggles that aren't reflected in a CRM. AI can suggest that the economic buyer is the key decision-maker, but a seasoned seller knows that real power might lie elsewhere, often with someone who doesn't even show up in the buying committee notes. Selling isn't just about convincing the right people; it's about knowing who the right people actually are.

Trust-based objections are another area where AI falls short. AI can generate a well-crafted response to concerns about scalability, reliability, or support, but trust isn't built on scripted answers. It's built on credibility and human connection. A prospect might express skepticism about a company's ability to handle their needs. AI will recommend data-driven reassurance. A great seller, on the other hand, will tell a story: something real, something that resonates on a deeper level.

Negotiation is another major blind spot for AI. It can analyze pricing trends, but it doesn't recognize the subtle signals that indicate when a buyer is bluffing or when they're willing to make concessions. AI might suggest a standard discount based on historical data, but a skilled negotiator knows when to hold firm and when to adjust the offer strategically. The difference between winning a deal at full value and leaving money on the table often comes down to reading the situation in real time—something AI simply can't do.

And then there's the long game: account vision. AI is designed to optimize short-term deal closure, but the best sales professionals think years ahead. They know when to push an upsell and when to wait, when to invest in a relationship and when to let it breathe. AI might recommend an immediate cross-sell opportunity, but a human seller recognizes that holding off and building further credibility will lead to a much larger deal down the road.

Lessons from AI-Driven Sales Failures

These gaps aren't just theoretical. Sales teams that rely too heavily on AI often find themselves losing deals they should have won. AI can push deals forward based on intent signals, but when procurement gets involved, those deals can die in red tape. It can automate outreach, but if a competitor takes the time to build real relationships, they'll win the business. It can suggest the "optimal" negotiation move, but if that move lacks human intuition, it can cost the deal.

The Room Goes Quiet

One company experienced this firsthand when AI-driven automation treated a high-value client as just another lead. The outreach was perfectly timed and the messaging precise, but it lacked depth. Meanwhile, a competitor took a different approach by investing time in personal conversations, understanding the client's long-term goals, and positioning themselves as a trusted partner. When it came time to make a decision, the client chose the company that had built the relationship, not the one that had optimized the email sequence.

Another case involved AI misreading a deal's momentum. AI flagged a champion as highly engaged, pushing the deal forward aggressively. But what it missed was the fact that procurement hadn't even been looped in yet. The deal stalled, internal politics took over, and what should have been a simple close turned into an uphill battle that never ended. A human seller, recognizing the potential roadblocks early, would have taken a more strategic approach: proactively addressing the unseen hurdles before they became deal-killers.

How to Use AI Without Losing Your Edge

The best sales professionals don't reject AI—they master it. AI should be used to handle the mechanics of selling, freeing up time for what actually wins deals: strategic execution and human connection.

AI can help score leads, generate proposals, and highlight potential risks, but sellers should always validate those insights with real-world judgment. AI can provide deal coaching, but execution should always be guided by human intuition. The moment sellers start relying on AI for relationship-building, negotiation, or navigating company politics, they lose their edge.

Trust is built through conversations, not through algorithms. Influence is earned through credibility, not through automation. The best salespeople will use AI as a tool to make them sharper, faster, and more informed, but they will never mistake it for a substitute for the skills that truly drive success.

William Anderson

AI is powerful. But when it comes to winning deals, the most powerful tool in sales is still you. The future of service sales isn't a race between humans and AI. It's a partnership where the tools do the heavy lifting, and we bring the wisdom, timing, and courage to use them with care.

The Room Goes Quiet

Chapter 31: The Augmented Seller: Using AI Without Losing Trust

The tools will always change. Today it is AI. Tomorrow it will be something else. What doesn't change is the seller. It isn't the tools that matter. It's how you use them.

Every generation of sellers has been handed something new—CRM systems, analytics platforms, automation engines. Some became sharper because of them. Others leaned too hard on the tools and lost the trust of their buyers. The pattern is clear: the best sellers absorb new capabilities without letting them replace the human edge.

AI is simply the latest and most powerful of those tools. It can sift through reports in seconds, analyze patterns across dozens of deals, and draft a recap before you leave the parking lot. Those capabilities are here now, not someday. But none of them replace what happens in the room when silence stretches and risk hangs in the air.

The Danger

AI creates speed and efficiency. Confuse that with credibility, and you lose the deal. Executives don't care that you mined their social profiles or generated a script that sounds empathetic. They care whether you understand their risk and have the discipline to stand with them if it fails.

Ask yourself, *Am I using this tool to get closer to the buyer's reality—or to hide from it?* If it's the latter, stop.

Never let AI be your mask. It is not there to make you sound polished. It is there to make you prepared, so that when you speak, your words have weight. If you use AI to shortcut trust, you'll sound like every other seller reading from a script. And scripted sellers lose.

The Opportunity

Services sales demands heavy preparation. You research industries, map stakeholders, spot risks, and draft briefs—all before you sit down with a customer. AI can reduce that burden and create space for execution where it matters most: in the room.

Think of AI as your research analyst, your pattern spotter, and your junior note-taker. It clears the noise so you can put your focus where it belongs—reading signals, carrying risk, and structuring commitments.

- Prep: AI can process filings, transcripts, and market reports in minutes. It can highlight financial pressures, anticipate objections, and map stakeholder networks. But that is only raw input. Your job is to convert it into insights and strategy for the specific room you'll walk into
- Analysis: AI can identify patterns across your deals— where opportunities stall, which objections recur, what risks surface repeatedly. Those patterns give you foresight. Execution is turning that foresight into structured commitments before silence tests you
- Post-call support: Let AI draft recaps, option maps, and next steps. Then refine them into something sharp and clear. The value is not in the draft—it is in your judgment, shaping it into a message the customer can act on

The opportunity is not speed for its own sake. It is what you do with the time and space AI creates.

The Human Edge

If all it took to win was perfect data or flawless notes, the best seller would already be a machine. That is not how deals close.

Deals close when someone carries the risk. When they hold silence with authority. When they tell the truth the buyer doesn't

The Room Goes Quiet

want to hear. Don't confuse being informed with being effective. A tool can make you informed. Only you can be trusted.

Every time you lean on AI, ask yourself, *What part of this deal can only be done by me?* The answer is always the same: silence, empathy, judgment, and risk ownership. Guard those moments. AI supports you. It does not replace you.

What Endures

AI doesn't replace the seller. It amplifies the seller who already owns the risk. The weak seller will use it to look polished and still lose. The strong seller will use it to prepare, to analyze, to support execution—and will win.

The tools will keep evolving. But the fundamentals will not. Trust, risk, execution, and scale have outlasted every shift in technology. They will outlast this one.

The lesson has nothing to do with software. The tool is never the edge. The seller is.

William Anderson

Chapter 32: Adapting Services Sales to Modern Revenue Recognition Models

The way businesses track and manage revenue is evolving, and for services sales leaders, this shift is more than just a financial adjustment. It's an operational and cultural transformation. Traditional services sales models, built around one-time projects, milestone-based revenue, and time-and-materials engagements, are giving way to financial frameworks that prioritize predictability, scalability, and long-term customer relationships.

This chapter isn't a finance lecture. It's a playbook for navigating a sales reality where the structure of the deal can directly impact the company's ability to grow, retain customers, and report revenue. Sales professionals who understand the rules, not just the relationships, create less friction and unlock faster paths to value.

To illustrate:

A senior account executive closed a massive $1.2M fixed-fee consulting deal, celebrated the win, and handed it to delivery. But finance stepped in. The deal's structure violated revenue recognition policy. Because services were front-loaded but billing was back-loaded, leadership couldn't recognize the revenue this quarter—or next. What looked like a win turned into a strategic setback.

New Revenue Recognition Models and Their Impact on Services Sales

The rise of annual contract value (ACV), total contract value (TCV), and annual recurring revenue (ARR) reflects this shift. These models align well with subscription-based services, managed service offerings, and consumption-driven pricing. However, they also create tension with the core value of services: solving customer problems efficiently and enabling them to move forward without creating long-term dependency.

For services sales teams, this creates both opportunities and challenges. It forces organizations to rethink how they sell, deliver, and measure success, while ensuring the move toward recurring revenue does not undermine the fundamental role of services: driving customer outcomes, not just selling contracts.

Annual Contract Value (ACV)

ACV represents the value of a contract over one year, excluding any one-time fees. It provides an annualized view of customer contracts, making it easier to forecast recurring revenue and track revenue growth over time.

ACV impacts services sales in the following ways:

- Encourages multiyear agreements, making long-term engagements more predictable
- Changes compensation structures, spreading payouts over time
- Alters service delivery expectations, aiming to sustain value continuously

Let's look at an example of shifting from fixed-fee to ACV-based engagements. A cloud migration firm that once offered a $600,000 fixed-fee engagement now sells it as a three-year managed service at $200,000 per year. This includes optimization, monitoring, and governance, not just delivery.

Sales teams had to make some key adjustments. Among these were recognizing that buyers want cost predictability and ongoing outcomes, not upfront spend. In terms of pipeline management, they needed to realize that revenue will be booked over time, not at close.

Meanwhile, services teams needed to adjust as well. Sustained performance became critical because renewals depend on continuous value, not just closing the loop. As well, expansion became proactive; teams must drive relevance beyond the original scope.

Leading Sales Teams Through This Transition

This isn't just about revenue math—it's about how sales organizations work.

Sales leaders face a lot of challenges. The top ones are:

- Short-term expectations vs long-term models
- Resistance to new compensation structures
- Need for tight alignment with post-sales success

Redefining Sales Metrics and Performance Management

Sales teams can't succeed in a new model if they're judged by old metrics. The KPIs must evolve.

Key Adjustments

- ACV growth: Tracks year-over-year customer revenue growth
- Net revenue retention (NRR): Measures account health via renewals, upsells, and expansions
- Expansion revenue: Incentivizes deepening customer value, not just opening the door

Example: Reframing Success

Previously, a sales rep marked the close of a $1 million consulting deal as a major success. Now, success looks like:

- $300,000 first-year engagement growing into a $700,000 renewal in year two
- $400,000 ARR growing into $600,000 ARR via added services
- 95% renewal rate on managed service contracts

The Room Goes Quiet

Adjusting Compensation and Incentives

Compensation drives behavior. When incentives are misaligned, even the best strategy will falter. Too often, companies cling to outdated compensation models that reward activity in the wrong place, encouraging sellers to chase quick wins while neglecting long-term value. If you want your sales culture to evolve, you must evolve the way people are paid.

One effective adjustment is to split commissions across the customer lifecycle. Instead of rewarding the seller entirely at contract signature, a better approach is to structure payouts in stages. For example, 40 percent of the commission might be paid when the deal closes, 30 percent when an adoption milestone is met, and the remaining 30 percent when the contract renews. This change ties seller success to customer success. It makes clear that closing the deal is only the beginning, and that revenue is fully earned only when the customer realizes value and chooses to stay.

Another lever is the bonus structure. If bonuses are tied only to new sales, sellers will naturally focus on landing fresh accounts. But when bonuses are tied to renewals, expansions, and multiyear agreements, the focus shifts toward long-term customer health. Sellers begin to think like owners rather than hunters. They plan accounts with an eye on durability, and they collaborate more with delivery teams because their own earnings depend on adoption and retention.

Consider the experience of one company that moved from one-time licenses to a subscription model. At first, the sales team carried their old habits forward. They still chased new deals, celebrated contract signatures, and then handed customers off. Renewals lagged, adoption was uneven, and expansions stalled. Leadership recognized that the problem was not motivation, but structure. They redesigned incentives so that renewals and expansions carried equal weight with new deals. Within a year, multiyear agreements rose by 15 percent, churn dropped by 20 percent, and collaboration between sales and services became visible in account planning sessions. What had once been a handoff culture started to look more like a shared mission.

The lesson is simple. If you want sellers to behave like partners, you must pay them like partners. Compensation tells your team what the company truly values. Aligning incentives with adoption, renewal, and expansion does more than shift numbers on a spreadsheet. It builds conviction that the seller's job is not just to sell, but to ensure that the customer succeeds. That is how you create accountability, reduce friction, and sustain growth.

Tactics for Leading Through the Shift

Service sales teams that embrace ACV, TCV, and ARR will gain predictable revenue, deeper customer relationships, and measurable, long-term business value. But to achieve this, sales leaders must redefine success to reflect recurring revenue realities, align comp plans to reward sustained value, equip teams to build trust over time, not just close fast, and bridge sales and customer success as a single revenue engine.

This is more than financial evolution. It's a strategic transformation. The teams that adapt will build systems that reward both trust and performance—and will become essential to the long-term success of their organizations.

Case Study: The Sales Rep, the Spreadsheet, and the RevRec Reckoning

Eli was a top-performing services rep. He was sharp, persuasive, and the kind of person who could sell backup generators during a blackout and still get five-star reviews. He knew how to close big deals and, more importantly, how to make them feel big.

So when he signed a $1.8 million transformation engagement with a global logistics company, he walked into the forecast call like a conquering hero. His sales manager, Lorna, gave him a nod of approval. Delivery was cautiously optimistic. Even the AE on the account said, "That's going to be a banner deal."

Then the SOW landed in revenue recognition (RevRec).

Two days later, Eli and Lorna found themselves on a call with Sam from RevRec—calm, composed, and wielding his spreadsheet with surgical precision.

Sam smiled politely. "Hey Eli, great work on the deal. But we have a few concerns."

He shared his screen. The spreadsheet lit up with red flags like a compliance-themed Christmas tree.

"The way this is structured," Sam said, "we can only recognize $200,000 for this fiscal year. The rest hits too late, and there's no clean milestone alignment."

Eli frowned. "But we've got signatures. Eighteen-month timeline. It's in the CRM."

"Right," Sam replied. "Booked. Not recognized. That's the difference between celebration and a board-level audit."

What Went Wrong
Eli had treated the deal like a traditional win, and he:

- Bundled advisory, execution, and managed services into one fixed-fee blob
- Set delivery to start late in the quarter
- Offered no measurable milestones or separate delivery components

In a previous world, he'd have been a hero. In an ACV- and ARR-driven model with real revenue policy controls, he was an accidental rule-breaker.

What They Did Next
Lorna, seeing where this was headed, stepped in to coordinate the fix with Sam and delivery.

Together, they:

- Broke the deal into three clean phases with scoped deliverables and clear timelines
- Front-loaded a rapid assessment sprint to start value realization immediately
- Recast ongoing support as a managed service with monthly reporting to unlock ARR classification

They also redesigned Eli's commission:

- 40% at contract signature
- 30% at first milestone completion
- 30% at the twelve-month renewal or NRR target hit

Eli didn't lose a dollar. But now his payout reflected how the company was actually evaluated.

Why It Worked
This wasn't a one-off patch. It became a template for how services deals should be built:

The Room Goes Quiet

- Revenue recognition got clean documentation, phase-based alignment, and confidence in compliance
- Sales got a commission structure and long-term incentives
- Delivery got clear swim lanes and milestone-driven accountability

More importantly, the deal supported the company's transition to ACV-based forecasting, NRR tracking, and value realization framing.

Eli, to his credit, didn't sulk. He adjusted.

By the fourth quarter, he was helping other sellers rework their opportunities *before* they landed in Sam's inbox.

Reflection
This is what adapting looks like.

Today's service sellers don't just pitch and close. They structure, align, and sequence value in a way that the entire business can support.

Deals like Eli's don't fail because they lack customer need. They fail when sellers treat financial structure as someone else's problem.

Modern selling isn't just about signing faster. It's about recognizing smarter.

Or as Sam from RevRec now likes to say:

"You can close the deal. But I close the books."

Chapter 33: The Margin Mindset – Why Sales Must Care About Profitability

The Myth of "Great Deals"
Eli thought he had just closed the perfect deal—$1.2 million in services, all signed, scoped, and submitted. The customer was thrilled. Delivery was prepared. Everyone on the sales team applauded.

But then the RevRec team flagged it. Margin contribution, they said, was under 5%. A deal that looked like a win to sales was a financial liability to the business.

It's a scenario that plays out more often than most teams admit. The symptoms are familiar: ballooning delivery hours, back-channel change requests, unexpected overtime, and awkward leadership conversations that start with, "Why didn't anyone catch this sooner?"

The root cause? Most sales teams are trained to chase revenue, not recognize risk.

What Is Operating Margin—And Why It Matters to Sales
Operating margin isn't just a metric for finance. It's the trailing indicator of how well your team has executed.

In services, it reflects what's left after the real work is done: delivery costs, support effort, coordination, and the grind that begins once the contract is signed. If revenue is the promise, operating margin is the reality.

And in a services-led world, that reality is dynamic. Margin is not a fixed number; it flexes based on the structure of the deal, the stability of the scope, and the discipline with which work is delivered.

The Room Goes Quiet

For sales professionals, this means their decisions—how they price, scope, and position the deal—have a direct line to the company's ability to invest in future growth. Discounting without structure? That's margin gone. Overpromising delivery timelines? Margin gone. Throwing "just one more thing" into the scope to win favor? Margin and trust gone.

It's not about saying no. It's about knowing what "yes" really costs.

High Revenue does not equal Victory

Big revenue numbers look good on CRM dashboards and board reports. But those numbers can be deceiving.

A services business can stack up bookings, celebrate top-line wins, and still find itself underwater, struggling to invest, unable to retain talent, and forced into cost-cutting cycles that demoralize teams and stall innovation.

High revenue with low margin is like a beautiful car with no fuel. It looks powerful. It just doesn't go very far.

That's why margin isn't just a finance conversation. It's a sales leadership discipline. It's how you protect your team's future, earn credibility with delivery, and build deals that don't just close but succeed.

When revenue is king and margin is ignored, you see symptoms fast:

- Customer escalations surge
- Renewals falter
- Delivery teams burn out
- Strategic initiatives get deferred

And the saddest part? The deals that caused the damage often looked like wins until someone checked the math.

Margin-Aware Sales Professionals Win More Than Deals

There's a sharp difference between sellers who chase deals and sellers who run businesses inside the business.

The latter understands margin. They know that pricing isn't just a negotiation tool, but a reflection of confidence and value. They know that scope isn't just a slide, but a promise. They understand that how a deal is structured has downstream consequences for teams they may never meet, but who will be held accountable for execution.

Margin-aware sales professionals:

- Price with clarity and defend value under pressure
- Partner with delivery to scope work that's both ambitious and doable
- Win the trust of finance because their deals hold up under scrutiny

These are the sellers who get pulled into larger accounts, asked to coach others, and invited to shape how their companies sell—not just what they sell.

In a services business, margin-aware sellers don't just win deals. They win influence.

The Four Pillars in Action

This isn't just about financial metrics. It's about reinforcing the core of effective services sales.

- Execution: High-margin deals are built on clean scope, solid estimates, and delivery alignment. They're not rescues, they're runway.
- Empathy: Knowing what delivery will face helps the seller empathize not just with the customer's needs, but with their own internal teams.
- Ownership: Margin discipline signals that the seller

The Room Goes Quiet

owns more than a number; they own the full arc of success.
- Value: Value isn't just what the customer receives. It's what the business retains after delivering it well.

Each of these pillars strengthens when margin is considered from the first conversation.

The Mindset Shift

This isn't about turning sellers into accountants. It's about raising the bar of what we define as a successful deal.

Anyone can sell something. But it takes discipline and perspective to sell something that works for the customer, for delivery, and for the business.

This mindset shift doesn't slow sellers down. It sharpens their edge. It earns them trust, builds strategic awareness, and positions them to thrive in organizations that care not just about closing but about executing.

Chapter 34: Protecting Margin in the Field – Pricing, Scope & Delivery Strategy

Where Margin Is Lost First: In the Deal Room

Most margin loss doesn't happen in delivery. It happens long before the first resource is staffed, before kickoff slides are built, before the ink is dry.

It happens when a deal is scoped "just to get it signed."

When a discount is given "just to hit this quarter."

When a change request process is skipped because "it's not a big ask."

The problem is that these shortcuts don't stay contained. They echo.

Delivery inherits a promise they didn't shape.

Finance inherits a deal they can't explain.

And the sales team, while celebrating the win, unknowingly compromised their own future renewals.

Margin protection doesn't start with spreadsheets—it starts with structure.

From Discounting to Value-Based Pricing

Discounts are fast. They're seductive. And they're expensive.

When you drop the price without changing what you deliver, you're cutting directly into the margin. The service still takes the same hours, the same effort, the same risk. But now you're

The Room Goes Quiet

doing it for less and sometimes much less.

The alternative isn't stubborn pricing. It's strategic pricing.

Value-based pricing means anchoring the deal around the *impact* delivered, not the input consumed. It means understanding what this service enables for the customer and pricing accordingly.

If the engagement saves the customer a million dollars, makes them faster in the market, or de-risks a strategic launch, then a premium price is more than fair. It's aligned.

To make this stick in practice:

- Start early: Value conversations need to happen before procurement enters the room.
- Use tools: ROI models, peer benchmarks, and outcome case studies help customers connect price to results.
- Avoid solo concessions: Any discount given should be paired with a concession in return: longer term, broader scope, and faster signature.

The best sales professionals don't just defend pricing. They own the narrative of value.

Structuring for Sustainability

A good deal isn't just winnable. It's executable.

That means building engagements that protect both customer success and internal efficiency. It means asking: will this deal make sense two months from now, when the team is in the thick of delivery?

Key strategies:

- Modular scopes: Break engagements into phased outcomes with measurable gates. This makes risk easier to manage and performance easier to prove.

- **Standardized offers:** Reuse what works. Standardization isn't rigidity. It is a repeatable success. Bundled offerings with defined scope, timelines, and pricing protect margin and accelerate sales cycles.
- **Clear scope boundaries:** Every engagement should have a finish line. Ambiguity kills margin. Define what's in, what's not, and how changes will be handled.

Think of structure as a service: it protects the customer's outcome and the delivery team's time.

Controlling Scope Without Killing Trust

Scope creep rarely looks like a threat at first. It usually arrives softly.

A customer asks, "Can we just add this one task?"

Or, "Can your team join this other meeting—it's related."

And before long, what was a 200-hour engagement is now at 280 and still climbing.

Scope creep kills margin and crushes trust, but it's often the seller who unintentionally sets the trap. When boundaries aren't clear from the start, or worse, when sellers blur them to seem accommodating, customers follow suit.

Instead:

- **Set expectations clearly:** At kickoff, walk through the scope together. Confirm what's included and what isn't.
- **Use language that empowers:** Rather than saying "no," say "yes, and here's how we'd scope that as

The Room Goes Quiet

an add-on."

- Coach delivery teams: Give them permission and language to escalate when scope shifts before it's too late.

Trust isn't about saying yes to everything. It's about delivering exactly what was promised, with excellence.

Balancing Resource Capacity with Pipeline Ambition

Selling without understanding delivery capacity creates downstream chaos. It leads to teams being overloaded, new hires rushed, or worse, burnout disguised as utilization.

The solution is shared visibility:

- Joint planning: Sales and delivery should review the pipeline regularly. Not just for headcount, but for skill alignment and timing.
- Balanced motion: Pair large transformation engagements with smaller, high-margin packages to smooth delivery load.
- Capacity signaling: Let delivery flag when bandwidth tightens, and let sales reprioritize accordingly. That's what partnership looks like.

High-margin organizations don't just close deals. They pace them.

Empowering Sellers to See the Full Picture

Many sellers never see what happens after the deal. They don't know how scope got stretched, or which resource had to pick up weekend hours, or how many additional meetings the project manager was asked to run.

It's not malice. It's separation.

The best way to fix it? Close the loop.

- Invite sales into postmortems, especially when deals go off track
- Share delivery wins and lessons learned in sales huddles
- Give sales tools to estimate deal profitability in real time, not after the fact

When sellers see the downstream, they shape deals upstream.

Margin Is a Team Sport

Sales doesn't own margin alone. Neither does delivery. But when one side operates without the other, the margin always suffers.

This chapter isn't about slowing down. It's about selling smarter—framing value, defending structure, and building engagements that win twice: at the point of sale, and again in execution.

The next time a deal gets shaped, pause and ask:

Is this something we can sell, deliver, and learn from, or just something we're trying to close?

Margin is the result. Structure is the behavior that gets you there.

Chapter 35: Margin as Strategy - Executive Levers for Scalable Profitability

The Misleading Safety of Revenue Growth

From the outside, the services business looked strong. Quarterly bookings were up. Headcount had increased. The teams were busy. On paper, everything pointed to momentum.

But inside the boardroom, the tone was different.

Revenue was climbing—but operating margin was shrinking. Free cash flow was tightening. Delivery burnout was rising. Leadership couldn't fund innovation or invest in long-term initiatives. Every dollar earned was already spoken for.

This wasn't a business scaling. It was sprinting in place.

The uncomfortable truth: revenue growth without margin growth is a slow leak that eventually becomes a break. And no amount of pipeline solves it.

Why Executives Must Prioritize Margin — Not Just Revenue

Revenue is a necessary condition for growth. But it's not a sufficient one.

Operating margin is what allows a company to invest, retain talent, weather market swings, and fund its own transformation. It's the core indicator of whether a services business is sustainable or simply high-velocity and fragile.

Too often, margin is treated as finance's responsibility. But in services, margin is organizational. Every deal shaped, every resource planned, every scope decision cascades into financial health or erosion.

Executives who lead with margin discipline:

- Create predictability in cash flow
- Increase valuation in the eyes of investors and acquirers
- Earn trust with delivery, sales, and finance, all pulling in the same direction

It's not about austerity. It's about alignment.

Redesigning Compensation to Reward Profitability

What you pay for is what people prioritize.

If a sales team earns full commission regardless of margin, they'll optimize for speed and volume. If they're rewarded for contribution, not just contract size, they'll sell differently.

Margin-focused compensation doesn't punish success. It clarifies what kind of success matters.

Key approaches:

- Tie variable compensation to margin contribution, not just revenue closed
- Incentivize multiyear value with rewards for renewals and expansions, not just land-and-leave deals
- Disincentivize deep discounting by requiring executive approval or splitting commission with delivery/finance

The goal isn't to micromanage. It's to create clarity, so that winning a deal and growing the business aren't in conflict.

Building Financial Acumen Across Teams

Most delivery teams don't think about contribution margin. Most sales teams don't understand the cost of goods sold. And that's the problem.

Margin protection begins when teams can see the impact of their choices:

- Train sales and delivery leaders on margin mechanics: what drives it, what kills it, and how to spot risk in real time
- Give deal teams access to profitability modeling tools: they can scenario-plan before committing
- Host shared deal reviews with finance, sales, and delivery: not to assign blame, but to build alignment

You don't need everyone to become a finance expert. You just need them to care enough to ask the right questions.

And that starts with understanding what's at stake.

Investing in Scalable Service Models

One of the most powerful margin levers is delivery model design.

Organizations that depend entirely on manual, bespoke execution find themselves trapped in a margin ceiling. Growth means headcount. Headcount means cost. And that model doesn't bend, it breaks.

High-performing services businesses invest in scale:

- Modular, productized offerings that can be reused, optimized, and delivered faster
- Digital accelerators that increase quality and reduce effort
- AI-powered tools to assist with discovery, scoping, reporting, and delivery tasks
- Self-service platforms that shift low-value interactions out of high-cost channels

This isn't just about automation. It's about strategic repeatability. If every deal requires reinvention, margins will always hover near zero.

If every deal reinforces something the business already does well, margin becomes a flywheel.

Enabling Real-Time Margin Visibility

Most services organizations track margin retrospectively: after the quarter ends, after the hours are spent, after the damage is done.

But margin is a leading indicator when monitored correctly.

Executives should invest in:

- Live dashboards that show margin by customer, offer, and region
- Forecasting tools that blend sales pipeline with resource capacity and scope risk
- KPI alignment across teams: contribution margin, NRR, and engagement profitability, not just bookings

When margin is visible, it becomes actionable.

And when it's actionable, it becomes cultural.

The Role of the Executive: Make Margin Everyone's Responsibility

Executives don't need to control every deal. But they do need to shape the ecosystem in which those deals are created.

That means:

- Designing compensation plans that reinforce profitable behavior

The Room Goes Quiet

- Resourcing teams to sell and deliver efficiently
- Investing in platforms and people that scale
- Holding leaders accountable for both growth *and* profitability

And above all, it means modeling the mindset and asking, not just "What did we close?" but "Did it move the business forward sustainably?"

Margin Is a Growth Engine

Profitability isn't the enemy of growth. It's what funds it.

The services organizations that win in the next decade won't be the ones with the most logos or the most bookings. They'll be the ones that understand how to structure success: deal by deal, dollar by dollar, and margin point by margin point.

Because in a services business, margin is more than a number.

It's the difference between staying alive and scaling up.

William Anderson

Case Study: Margin Discipline in the Field: Two Paths, Two Outcomes

The Setup: When Margin Is Everyone's Job—or No One's

Altura Systems and Northbeam Consulting both entered the services market with ambition. Both sold to enterprise IT buyers. Both built strong delivery teams and had technical credibility.

But five years later, one company was quietly bleeding margin while the other was thriving with rising rates and strategic customer loyalty.

The difference wasn't in talent, market, or methodology.

It was in who owned the margin—and when.

Altura Systems: The Slow Decline of Margin Awareness

Altura's consulting arm was created to support software adoption. Services were considered a complement: valuable but secondary to the core business of licensing and renewals.

From the start, operating margin was framed as a leadership metric:

- VPs and senior directors were compensated on margin
- Margin was measured at the regional level and diluted across all projects
- Sales reps were compensated on bookings alone, with no tie to deal quality
- Delivery had limited input in the deal-shaping process

The Room Goes Quiet

At first, this didn't seem like a problem. Deals moved fast. Targets were hit.

But the early signs of erosion were already present.

Discounts, once a tactical move to unlock a deal, became the default. Sellers offered them automatically, often before the customer pushed. Larger discounts were used as the lead argument, an easy way to compete and a substitute for a compelling narrative.

Scope began to blur. Deals were designed to close, not to succeed. Details got fuzzy. Delivery risk was overlooked in favor of speed. Services were presented as flexible, forgiving, and endlessly available—until they weren't.

And when problems surfaced?

The solution was simple:

"Just throw in some free work."

"Run a few extra workshops—off the books if needed."

It became routine. Customers expected extras. Delivery absorbed the cost.

By year three, services bookings slowed. Quotas got harder to achieve. And quietly, a dangerous belief spread among the field:

"We're too expensive for what we offer."

Not because the services weren't valuable, but because no one knew how to defend them anymore. Years of discounting had trained the market—and the sellers—that concessions were standard, and value was optional.

Delivery teams grew frustrated. Margins collapsed.

Executives saw the trend in the numbers, but the damage was already done.

Altura didn't ignore the margin.

They just failed to make it anyone's responsibility at the moment that mattered.

And when that happens, the margin always disappears.

Northbeam Consulting: Profitability as a Sales Culture
Northbeam took a different path. They were a standalone consulting firm with no attached product and no fallback revenue. Profitability wasn't a secondary concern. It was the business.

From day one, they made a clear decision. Margin would be a shared responsibility:

- Frontline sellers were compensated on project-level gross margin
- Regional leaders owned territory margin targets
- The national VP of sales was comped on overall operating margin

This wasn't just a KPI shift. It was a culture shift.

Sellers were trained in financial mechanics. They used margin calculators in real time. They learned how to scope deals with delivery, not around them. When customers pushed back on price, sellers didn't flinch. They leaned into the value conversation, armed with outcomes, not discounts.

Where Altura trained buyers to expect concessions, Northbeam trained theirs to expect quality.

Sellers at Northbeam didn't apologize for pricing.

They stood behind it because they knew it worked.

They'd seen the customer results. They trusted the scope. They partnered with delivery from the start.

The Room Goes Quiet

And most importantly, they knew their compensation depended on structuring the deal right, not just getting it signed.

As a result:

- Northbeam's average deal margin rose year over year
- Customer expansion grew consistently
- Sellers started describing their own offers as "elite," and customers agreed

Even in tough negotiations, sellers didn't reach for the discount lever.

They reached for proof. And that difference—the confidence in value—became self-reinforcing.

Two Models with Two Outcomes.

	Aultura Systems	**Northbeam Consulting**
Who owns the Margin	VIPs and senior directors only	Sellers, regional leaders, VPs
Sales compensation tied to margin	No	Yes, at the project level
Discounting behavior	Default and habitual	Rare and value-justified
Perception of services	"Too expensive"	"Premium and elite"
Delivery morale	Reactive and burdened	Confident and engaged
Customer Mindset	Expecting extras	Expecting outcomes

William Anderson

Lesson: You Can't Course-Correct Margin After the Deal is Done.

At Altura, margin was managed from the top down and was too far removed from deal execution to drive behavior.

At Northbeam, margin was operationalized. Everyone saw it. Everyone shaped it. Everyone benefited when it was protected.

The result?

One company struggled to defend its own value.

The other turned margin into its market advantage.

Chapter 36: The High Cost of Chasing the Clock

For as long as businesses have had sales teams, they have also had deadlines: end of quarter, end of year, and end of fiscal. These moments serve as key indicators of a company's health, provide predictable revenue reporting for investors, and structure the rhythm of the business itself. Meeting these milestones is not just important—it's essential. They determine stock prices, dictate funding for new initiatives, and impact the ability to hire and expand.

Yet, despite their necessity, these deadlines also create behaviors that ultimately erode long-term sales effectiveness, especially in services sales. They drive discounting patterns that damage profitability, create artificial urgency that misaligns with customer needs, and often result in rushed, poorly structured deals that lead to long-term delivery and execution problems.

For sales leaders and managers, walking the line between hitting critical business targets and avoiding the pitfalls of deadline-driven desperation is one of the most difficult balancing acts in the profession. The solution is not to ignore or resist deadlines but to manage them strategically, ensuring that end-of-quarter pressure doesn't become the defining factor in customer relationships or the way deals are structured.

The Cost of Arbitrary Deadlines in Sales

The Discounting Death Spiral

One of the most damaging consequences of rigid end-of-quarter or end-of-year sales pressures is the normalization of discounting as a primary closing tool. Customers quickly learn that sales teams become desperate as deadlines approach. If a buyer knows that a 15 percent discount is standard in the last week of a quarter, they will never pay full price again. Worse, procurement departments delay decisions until the next "desperation window" to drive even deeper discounts.

In services sales, the damage runs deeper. Every rushed deal isn't just risky—it's a margin leak waiting to happen. Unlike product sales, where a discount may simply reduce the revenue from a single transaction, services come with delivery costs that don't disappear just because the deal was closed at a lower price. Every dollar shaved off the price of a service engagement directly cuts into profitability, limits delivery capacity, and ultimately erodes the perceived value of the service.

Additionally, discounted services deals often come with rushed scoping, unrealistic expectations, and an execution burden that falls on delivery teams who had no part in setting the terms. A poorly sold services deal doesn't just impact revenue; it creates downstream execution failures that damage customer relationships, reduce renewal rates, and erode trust in the company's ability to deliver value.

The Illusion of Urgency: When the Clock Replaces the Customer's Needs

One of the most damaging side effects of managing sales to arbitrary deadlines is the creation of false urgency. When sales teams are pressured to close deals by the end of a quarter or fiscal year, they often manufacture urgency that doesn't align with the customer's actual priorities. This misalignment can erode trust, distort the natural buying cycle, and ultimately push customers into making poor decisions, or worse, delay purchasing altogether because they feel manipulated.

At its core, sales should be about solving problems. Customers buy when they recognize a compelling need, believe in the value of the solution, and trust that now is the right time to act. Yet, when urgency is driven by an internal sales timeline rather than customer needs, it becomes transparent that the seller's motivations are self-serving.

The Room Goes Quiet

Customers today are more informed than ever. They recognize sales tactics, understand procurement processes, and know that end-of-quarter discounts are often just a way for sellers to hit quota. When a salesperson insists that a deal "must be signed before the quarter ends," but the only reason is an internal deadline, it signals a lack of partnership and long-term thinking. Instead of feeling like a valued customer, the buyer feels like a means to an end.

This erosion of trust has long-term consequences. Even if the deal closes, the customer may later regret being pressured into the purchase, leading to buyer's remorse, increased scrutiny of the sales process, and a reduced likelihood of repeat business. Worse, they may delay their decision altogether, suspecting that an even better discount is coming next quarter.

For services sales, this problem is magnified. Services engagements require deep collaboration between sales, delivery teams, and the customer. If the deal is rushed to meet an arbitrary deadline, key scoping discussions may be skipped, critical details may be overlooked, and the customer's expectations may be mismanaged. A poorly scoped services deal doesn't just impact the seller. It sets up the delivery team for failure, strains the customer relationship, and can lead to dissatisfied clients who either abandon future renewals or demand costly rework.

The most effective sales organizations recognize the difference between real urgency and manufactured urgency. Customers will move faster when urgency is tied to their business needs—regulatory deadlines, competitive threats, budget cycles—not because a seller needs to close a deal by the end of the quarter.

The "Boom and Bust" Revenue Problem

Short-term deadline-driven selling also creates a feast-or-famine revenue cycle. If every deal is closed in the last few days of a quarter, the next quarter starts with an empty pipeline. Instead of building a steady, predictable sales rhythm, teams are constantly scrambling to rebuild their pipeline after each deadline rush. This rollercoaster effect makes accurate forecasting nearly impossible and increases stress across the organization.

In services sales, this issue compounds as delivery teams become overwhelmed with a sudden influx of new projects that all kick off at once, leading to resource allocation nightmares and degraded service quality. Worse, it leaves gaps in future revenue, forcing the same frantic behavior every quarter instead of creating a stable, scalable sales motion.

Breaking the Cycle: Managing Sales Without Deadline Desperation

The key to avoiding these pitfalls isn't to ignore deadlines but to make them irrelevant by building a healthy, well-structured pipeline that naturally balances deal flow over time. When a sales team consistently works on opportunities across multiple time horizons—this quarter, next quarter, and even next year—there is no sudden crunch at the end of a reporting period because deals are closing at a steady cadence.

Sales forecasting plays a critical role in this approach. When a sales team understands its pipeline beyond the current quarter, it removes the artificial need to push deals forward before they are ready. A well-structured pipeline provides predictable revenue flow, prevents last-minute discounting, and ensures that sellers are operating from a position of strength rather than desperation.

This requires discipline. Sales leaders must ensure that their teams are always engaging in pipeline development activities, not just when their quarterly numbers are at risk. Early-stage prospecting, nurturing long-term opportunities, and proactively creating new customer engagements should be standard, not crisis-driven.

The Room Goes Quiet

For managers, ensuring a steady, predictable pipeline is the best way to avoid artificial crunch periods. This starts with accurate forecasting, not just optimistic guesses at what might close, but a real understanding of which deals are progressing and which need more time. Regular deal reviews should focus not only on the current quarter but on building out future revenue as well.

Walking the Fine Line Between Business Targets and Smart Selling

Deadlines will always exist, and they will always matter. Investors, boards, and executives rely on these metrics to steer the company forward. But how these targets are pursued determines whether a business is building sustainable success or constantly chasing numbers in a way that undermines its long-term potential.

The most effective sales organizations ensure consistent pipeline coverage, align deal closures with customer needs rather than artificial urgency, and structure services sales in a way that protects delivery integrity. When sales teams stop relying on last-minute discounts and deadline pressure, and instead focus on steady, predictable deal flow, they not only hit their targets—they build a business that is stronger, more profitable, and far more resilient to the natural fluctuations of any given quarter.

Sales success isn't about just hitting numbers once. It's about creating a system that predictably delivers value while maintaining profitability and execution integrity. The best way to hit deadlines isn't to scramble to meet them, but to make them irrelevant.

William Anderson

Chapter 37: The Future of Service Sales – Adapting to a Changing Landscape

When you first opened this book, you weren't looking for tricks. You were looking for something deeper—a shift. A way to stop chasing the numbers and start owning the outcome.

Now, you've seen what that shift looks like in the field.

You've walked through the early missteps and hard pivots. You've seen what happens when sellers flinch on price, overscope out of fear, or rely on relationship alone. And you've seen what happens when they stop doing that and when they qualify with clarity, trade with discipline, and lead the room with presence.

But this isn't a static game. The pace of change is only accelerating.

AI is changing how customers buy, how internal politics unfold, and how influence gets measured. Business models are bending toward recurring revenue and margin intelligence. Platform thinking and ecosystem-based value are no longer strategy slides but operational mandates. And sellers who cling to what's worked in the past will not be outperformed. They'll be outclassed.

This isn't just about tools or trends. It's about the gravity of old habits.

Quarter-end pushes. Discount-first proposals. Leading with features. Hoping delivery figures it out after the ink dries. These aren't sales strategies. They're survival patterns, and they don't scale. You can't just drop them. You have to replace them with something stronger. Something cleaner. Something deliberate.

That's what this book was for.

The Room Goes Quiet

To show you that it's not just about services but about selling clarity in moments of confusion. Selling confidence in moments of pressure. Selling conviction in rooms where uncertainty used to win.

You've learned how to run discovery that earns respect before the slides. How to build trust without overpromising. How to shape opportunities with strategic empathy and close them with margin intact. You've seen what it takes to win a deal without losing your delivery team—or your reputation.

So now the question shifts.

Not "Do I know what to do?" but "What role will I play from here?"

Some will shelve this book, nod to the ideas, and slide back into the familiar grind. Others will take it forward. Not because they were told to, but because they saw a better way to sell—one that doesn't sacrifice the future to win the moment.

You might be the rep who finally stands firm when finance pressures a discount. The manager who rewrites qualification criteria so that risk and delivery are embedded from the start. The executive who stops measuring "what closed" and starts measuring "what lasted."

Wherever you sit, your influence starts now. Not with a mandate. With a model.

Show your team how service sales becomes more than a line item. Make it the lever for retention. For expansion. For real strategic impact.

And if you're still wondering whether any of this will actually work in the real world, remember Ace.

He didn't just win because he sold well. He won because he never forgot who he was there to protect.

William Anderson

When the Room Goes Quiet

The pursuit team walked in confidently. They had done everything right on paper. The deck was clean, the value proposition clear, the solution mapped directly to the client's goals. Roles were aligned, transitions practiced, objections anticipated. The sponsor had budget. Procurement was engaged. Everything pointed toward a win.

Until the room changed.

It happened on the last slide. The sponsor checked the time. The operations lead leaned back, arms folded. Procurement scribbled a note, then went still. And the executive—calm, curious, dispassionate—asked the question that never appears in RFPs: *What happens if you cannot deliver this?*

It was not a trap. It was not a challenge. It was the test.

The room did not get tense. It got quiet. Not confrontational. Not resistant. Just silent. The kind of silence that signals a decision is being made, not aloud but internally. The kind of silence that tells you this is the moment where confidence either transfers or disappears.

The team froze. No one stepped in. No one claimed the risk. No one answered the real question the customer was asking: *Can I trust you with this?*

A few days later, I got the call. They wanted a post-mortem. I knew the client, the dynamics, and the mechanics of the deal. But I also knew, before they finished explaining, that the loss had not happened in that final meeting. It had happened earlier, when they talked about capabilities but not consequences, when they scoped delivery but avoided ownership, when the service seller leaned on "the team" instead of taking point.

That silence had not been indecision. It had been rejection. The client did not say no. They simply did not hear anyone they

The Room Goes Quiet

could say yes to.

That is not easy feedback to receive, but soft landings do not teach you anything. I have seen this moment before, many times. I have stood in that room. I have heard that silence. And I have learned what it takes to hold your ground when trust is gone and the weight is shifting.

This is who the book is for. Not the high-pressure seller who chases contracts. Not the strategist who hides behind theory. Not the architect who scopes in a vacuum. It is for the professional who knows that selling services is not about what you say. It is about what you carry. It is about standing inside the risk, about being the voice in the room who says, *We will not let you fail, and here is why.*

I have spent years coaching teams through that moment. Helping them recognize the shift. Helping them hear the silence before it settles. Helping them step into it, not with defensiveness or ego but with clarity and calm. Because when the room goes quiet, there is no more time to build trust. You are either the one they believe in, or you are not.

And in that moment, someone has to speak. Not to fill the space, but to steady it. To make the commitment personal. To say, *You can put this on me.*

When someone says that and means it, the silence breaks. The deal moves. The relationship begins.

That is what I do. And that is what I challenge you to do. Not just to close more deals, but to earn the kind of trust that makes those deals worth closing. Own the moment. Own the outcome. And when the room goes quiet, be the one who brings it back to life.

Because in the end, the work that matters most does not go to the loudest voice. It goes to the one willing to carry it when everything else goes still.

The silence will come. What you do with it will define you.

William Anderson

Appendix: Tools, Frameworks, and Execution Models

This appendix is not an afterthought, but the practical backbone of the strategies you've just read. While the core chapters focused on mindset, narrative, and deal dynamics, what follows are repeatable tools and frameworks designed to help you *scale* those principles in real-world environments.

Whether you're a sales leader building a region-wide model, a practitioner refining your own motion, or an executive aligning delivery with go-to-market execution, this section gives you the structure to do it right, without reinventing the wheel.

Use this appendix to reinforce training, guide strategy sessions, or create clarity in moments where deals stall, complexity rises, or alignment slips. These are the blueprints that turn trust into scale.

What's Inside This Section:

- Building a Sales Maturity Model: From Small Teams to Enterprise Scalability – A progression framework to evaluate, align, and advance sales capability from tactical selling to strategic growth.
- Designing Tiered Service Offerings for Scalability – Tools for packaging services into clear, scalable offerings that protect margin and create expansion paths.
- Implementing a Customer Segmentation Model – A practical way to prioritize effort, tailor messaging, and structure engagements by customer profile and potential.
- Creating a Seamless Engagement Framework – A visual and operational blueprint for reducing friction across the sales-to-delivery handoff.
- Aligning Sales Strategy with Customer Success – A guide to integrating post-sale accountability into your

The Room Goes Quiet

GTM model, with metrics that reinforce lifetime value.

- Scaling with Structure: The Future of Service Sales – A closing synthesis of structural elements required to scale without eroding strategic depth or trust.
- AI in Service Sales: An Enablement Framework – A practical framework for integrating AI into sales enablement, discovery, and execution—without losing the human edge.

Building a Sales Maturity Model: From Small Teams to Enterprise Scalability

Service sales organizations evolve in stages. The tools, processes, and strategies that work for a five-person sales team are entirely different from those needed for a global enterprise. Organizations must understand where they are in their maturity model and implement the right tools accordingly.

The table below outlines a Service Sales Maturity Model, showing the common challenges and solutions at each level:

Sales Maturity Level	Characteristic	Common Challenges	Key Solution
Level 1: Small, Agile Sales Team	Founder driven, relationship-based sales with highly customized deals.	No standardizdation unpredictable revenue, long sales cycle.	Use basic CR tools, create repeatable service tiers, define entry-level offerings to reduce custom work
Level 2: Mid-market phasing scale	Increased deal volume requires standardizdation with playbooks and segmentation emerging.	Sales cycles vary in length, service scoping is inconsistent customer expectations are unclear.	Implemented tiered service offerings, develop customer segmentation models, integrate automated propsal generation.
Level 3: Enterprise Sales Engine	Highly structured sales process, AI and automation optimize customer engagement.	Scaling personalized engagements, account expansion and integrating AI-driven insights.	Use AI-powered CRM, defined engagement frameworks and implement automated lead scoring expansion models.

By recognizing which stage they are in, organizations can tailor their approach to move toward a scalable, repeatable sales model.

Designing Tiered Service Offerings for Scalability

A common challenge in service sales is the complexity of pricing and scoping engagements. Without clear structures, sales cycles drag on, deals get stalled, and customers struggle to understand what they're buying.

To solve this, tiered service offerings provide predefined engagement levels based on customer needs. This simplifies decision-making while maintaining flexibility.

Service Tier	Description	Ideal Customer	Typical Deliverables
Foundational Services	Entry-level engagements with low-risk, quick-starts services	small or new customers who need a starting point.	Readiness assessments, compliance reviews basic implementation support.
Advanced Solutions	More complex services with deeper customization	mid-market companies seeking optimization and intergation	Workflow automation, system integrations, process reengineering
Strategic Partnerships	High-touch advisory services and long-term engagements	Enterprises looking for continuos innovation and transformation	Executive advisory, managed services AI-driven optimization.

A digital transformation consulting firm, for example, might structure its services like this:

1. Baseline Readiness Assessment: A two-week analysis of existing infrastructure
2. Cloud Migration Strategy: A full implementation roadmap tailored to business needs
3. Ongoing AI-Driven Optimization: A long-term engagement where the provider continuously refines and enhances cloud usage

The Room Goes Quiet

By guiding customers through a natural progression, sales teams reduce friction, increase deal velocity, and create a structured path for long-term growth.

Implementing a Customer Segmentation Model

A one-size-fits-all sales approach is no longer effective. Service providers must tailor their sales strategy based on customer size, industry, and operational complexity.

The following table outlines a customer segmentation framework, helping sales teams focus on the right opportunities:

Customer Segment	Key Characteristic	Sales Focus	Best Service Offering
High-Growth Start-ups.	Fast-moving, budget-conscious, and need rapid deployment.	Emphasize speed, flexibility, and cost efficiency.	Entry-level solutions with minimal customization.
Mid-market Enterprises	Need scalable solutions, integrate with existing solutions.	Focus on ROI intrgration, and process optimization.	Modual service offerings that scale with their needs.
Global Corporations	Require enterprise-wide transformation, regulatory compliance	Position as long-term partners, drive continuous value	Strategic partnerships with dedicated account teams.

For example, a cybersecurity services firm might offer:

- Basic compliance packages for startups needing fast regulatory approvals
- Customized security frameworks for mid-market firms integrating with legacy systems
- AI-driven security monitoring for global enterprises requiring real-time threat detection

By aligning sales efforts with customer needs, organizations increase win rates, shorten sales cycles, and improve retention.

Creating a Seamless Engagement Framework

Winning a deal is just the first step. The real challenge is ensuring customers move through each stage of engagement successfully. Without a structured process, sales teams risk losing momentum after the contract is signed.

The customer engagement framework ensures a seamless transition across all touchpoints:

Engagement Stage	Key Focus	Priliminary Activity
Discovery	Align with business needs.	Initial consultation, and expectations. needs assessment, solution recommendations.
Implementation	Executing agreed upon services.	Deployment, integration, process redesign.
Optimization	Refining and evolving the engagement.	On-going AI improvements, advisory services, proactive enhancements.
Continuous Innovation	Expanding and evolving the engagement	On-going AI-improvements, advisory services, proactive enhancements.

For instance, a consulting firm specializing in AI-driven automation might:

1. Start with an AI-readiness assessment, mapping out business challenges
2. Implement an automation strategy, integrating AI tools into operations
3. Provide continuous improvement services, fine-tuning models based on real-world data

By having this framework in place, customers experience a structured, high-value journey that maximizes long-term success.

Aligning Sales Strategy with Customer Success

Service sales is no longer about closing a deal and moving on. The most successful organizations integrate customer success into their sales process, ensuring clients achieve measurable outcomes.

A cloud migration firm, for example, might begin by helping a client move workloads to the cloud, but instead of stopping there, it proactively identifies opportunities for security enhancements, automation strategies, and cost optimizations.

This continuous engagement model increases customer retention, drives expansion, and strengthens relationships over time.

Scaling with Structure: The Future of Service Sales

Sales teams that scale effectively move beyond instinct-based selling. They implement structured frameworks that enable repeatability, efficiency, and long-term customer alignment.

Small teams thrive on flexibility, but as they grow, they must adopt tiered service models, structured engagement frameworks, and AI-driven customer insights to maintain efficiency without losing their strategic edge.

The organizations that master these frameworks will not only close more deals but also create lasting partnerships that drive sustained revenue and market leadership.

AI in Service Sales: An Enablement Framework

(Note: This book is not about AI-driven service sales—that would be a book unto itself. Instead, this section provides a practical guide for how AI can be used to optimize service sales execution.)

AI does not replace relationships, trust, or consultative sales expertise, but it does enhance decision-making and reduce inefficiencies.

William Anderson

AI's Role in Service Sales:

AI Capability	Impact on Sales Service	How to Apply It
Customer Segmentation	Identifies high-value accounts and prioritizes outreach.	Use AI-driven CRM insights to target accounts with the highest probabilities of expansion.
Deal Predictibility Models	Analyzes past engagements to forecast close probabilites	AI-powered analytics can predict which deals are likely to stall and why
Dynamic Pricing Models	Adjust pricing based on deal conditions and competitor benchmarks.	AI-assisted pricing trools can recommend value-based pricing strategies in real time.
AI-Guided Sales Playbooks	Provides rea;t-time recommendations during sales calls.	AI can suggest talking points, case studies, and objective-handling tactics based on the customer profile.
Sentiment Analysis	Read customer emails and meeting transcripts to access deal health	AI can flag when customer engagement is dropping, signalling a potential stall.

The key to AI in service sales isn't automation—it's augmentation. AI won't replace human expertise, but those who leverage it will outperform those who don't.

Authors Note

This book came together in ways I did not fully expect. In many respects, I have been writing it my entire career. Thirty years of lessons, customer conversations, wins, and losses built the foundation. More recently, new tools helped me isolate and refine scattered thoughts, shape them into something clear, and push the work across the finish line.

I have written most of my life: high school essays, professional papers, blogs, and even unfinished books. The turning point came when I built the Service Sales Accelerator. I was asked a simple question: *How do we make other services sellers like you? How do we distill what makes you successful and pass that on?* That challenge set me on the path. The framework I created—twelve basic tactics—became the seed of the Accelerator and later the foundation of this book.

I was fortunate to have readers who gave their time and candor when the work felt too heavy. My alpha readers, Jennifer, Karen, Idalia, and others whose names I will no doubt recall after this is in print, pushed me to keep going. My wife, Julie, carried more of this book than anyone should, quietly absorbing the late nights, the frustration, and the obsessive dedication to consulting. My children, Idalia, Chris, and Bianca, and my friends endured the same, often putting up with my intensity and quirks. Their patience is something I will never take for granted.

I also owe thanks to the people who shaped me as a professional. Scott taught me that communication is not what you say, but what they hear. Derek and Rampi sharpened me during my years at ThruPoint. Dan forced me to see that if the business is not getting done, nothing else matters. Bob showed me that simply being good in this business has its own power. Craig has been more peer than boss, a sounding board whose perspective has made me better. Their influence is written into these pages.

William Anderson

Two people deserve special recognition for helping this book come alive. Vince, my friend and publisher, believed in the project from the beginning and gave me the push to put it into the world. Robyn, my editor, was a gift to find. She shaped the words here with care and precision I could not have achieved alone.

Most of all, I thank God for blessing me with the career I have had, the customers I have served, and the people I have been surrounded by. None of this would exist without His guidance.

This book reflects as much of them as it does of me. I hope it serves you as well as they have served me.

The Room Goes Quiet

Two people deserve special recognition for helping this book come alive. Vince, my friend and publisher, believed in the project from the beginning and gave me the push to put it into the world. Robyn, my editor, was a gift to find. She shaped the words here with care and precision I could not have achieved alone.

Most of all, I thank God for blessing me with the career I have had, the customers I have served, and the people I have been surrounded by. None of this would exist without His guidance.

This book reflects as much of them as it does of me. I hope it serves you as well as they have served me.

About the Author

William Anderson is a veteran of enterprise consulting and services sales, known for leading high-stakes pursuits where trust and execution matter most. He began his career serving in the U.S. Army, with the Pentagon as his primary duty station, before moving into consulting and sales leadership.

As part of Red Hat Consulting North America, he created the Service Sales Accelerator, a program that reshaped how sellers move beyond product pitches into outcome-driven conversations that win executive confidence. Across his career, he has also coached executive pursuit teams and advised senior leaders on building services-led strategies that align sales, delivery, and customer success. His thought leadership reaches a global audience through LinkedIn and Medium, where he writes on services, execution, AI strategy, and the behavioral side of selling. He also serves as an advisor and board member, helping organizations align go-to-market strategy, technology, and culture to deliver lasting impact.

Beyond his work, William values time with his wife and three children. He is an avid traveler and an enthusiastic cook, and he enjoys board games and tabletop wargaming as creative outlets for strategy and storytelling.

The Room Goes Quiet is his first book, bringing together decades of lessons on what it takes to win when risk is highest and silence decides the outcome.

For more of William's work and ongoing thought leadership, visit www.virtuosostrategy.com

INDEX

A

accelerated timelines, 117, 136
Accountability Models that Prevent Misalignment, 195
Account executives (AE), 58, 61, 185, 206, 233
ACV impacts services sales, 229
Adapting Services Sales, 6, 228
AI, 6, 12, 59, 186, 215, 218–27, 260, 267, 272–73
AI in Service Sales, 6, 220, 267, 272
Aisha, 104–8
Aligning Sales Strategy with Customer Success, 266, 271
alignment, 11, 13, 22, 24, 38–39, 42–43, 47, 56, 68, 83, 89, 99, 101, 123–24, 126–27, 141–42, 194–95, 197, 207, 219, 230, 246–47, 266
Altura, 250–53
  Altura Systems, 249–50
Anaya, 40–44
Anderson, William, 1, 3, 9–287
Anderson, Willian, 3
annual contract value (ACV), 228–29, 232–33
annual recurring revenue (ARR), 228, 230, 232
archetypes, 51–52, 55, 57
Architect archetypes, 59–60
architects, 53–54, 59, 61–63, 72, 188, 264

ARR (annual recurring revenue), 228, 230, 232
Augmented Seller, 6, 225
automation, 104–5, 107, 129, 181, 186, 215–17, 219–20, 223, 248, 267, 271–72
  check-in, 42–43
automation framework, 38, 188
automation strategies, 271

B

B2B sales, 89, 124
best practices, 117, 136, 189
best salespeople, 71, 76, 80, 88, 153, 215, 220, 222–23, 241
best teams, 111, 115
Breaking Down Silos Between Sales and Delivery, 184
building cases, 121
building engagements, 241, 244
Building Sustainable Success, 5, 180
building trust, 4–5, 25, 49, 93, 96, 193, 196
business, 3, 9, 24–25, 37, 50, 53, 58–59, 63, 82, 98–99, 120, 124–25, 132, 148–49, 175, 210, 222, 235–36, 238–39, 246, 248–49, 251, 255, 257, 259, 269–70, 274
  customers,' 216
business cases, 27, 117, 121, 136, 144
business decision, 92

business impact, 37, 105, 148, 152, 175, 177, 206
   long-term, 96
   real, 42, 153
business leaders, 208, 217–18
business models, 51, 58, 260
   platform-based, 216, 219
business objectives, 56, 126
business outcomes, 174
   measurable, 184
business partners, 84
business scaling, 245
business strategy, 175, 184
business value, 157
   long-term, 232
buyers, 10–15, 20–22, 27–29, 31–33, 35–37, 39, 45–47, 66–67, 69–70, 74–75, 89–94, 98–102, 124, 137, 139, 144–46, 151, 154, 156, 191, 203, 209, 220–22, 225–26, 229, 256–57
   economic, 175, 221
buyers carry risk, 101
buyers trust, 203

C

capabilities, 9–10, 19, 28, 33–34, 40, 46, 73–74, 98, 112, 114, 118–19, 209, 218, 220, 225, 263
   technical, 30, 37, 110, 122
capital, political, 7, 27–28
career, 71, 114, 187, 202, 204–5, 274–76
case study, 4–6, 12–13, 15, 32, 39–40, 72, 85, 99, 103, 126, 128, 139–40, 143–44, 148, 156, 170, 187, 198, 211, 220, 232, 249, 272
CFO, 16–18, 30, 66, 110–11, 120, 155, 171, 175
champion, 5, 15, 29, 31, 37, 45–47, 54, 66–67, 70–71, 93–94, 103, 108, 151–52, 154–56, 203, 211, 223
change ties seller success, 231
Changing Landscape, 5–6, 214, 260
CIO, 15–17, 27, 30, 38, 42, 69, 89, 125, 137
Claire, 144–46
client, 35, 50, 53–54, 60, 62, 83, 111–14, 118, 125–26, 144, 184, 218, 223, 263–64, 271
   new, 183
client executives, 57
Closers, 60, 62–63
cloud infrastructure, 128–29, 216
Cloud Migration Strategy, 269
cloud providers, 59
coach delivery teams, 243
collaborative qualification, 98, 100–101, 178
commitment, 5, 10, 24, 82, 103, 123–24, 126–28, 136, 139, 141, 143–46, 152, 178, 193, 195–96, 198, 209–10, 264
   contractual, 82
   informal, 81–82
   structuring, 94, 226
Commitment Beyond the Contract, 83

companies, 16, 25, 33, 50–51, 58, 60, 63, 68–69, 83, 86, 90, 102, 113, 120, 125–26, 133, 135, 147, 152, 156, 174, 183–85, 189, 194, 200, 215–19, 222–23, 231–32, 234, 238, 245, 249, 254–55, 268

  enterprise software, 178

  financial services, 128

  hybrid platform-consulting, 58

  logistics, 126, 232

  manufacturing, 85, 117, 144

compensation, 231–32, 246, 252–53

concessions, 93, 139, 146, 173, 176–77, 221–22, 241, 251–52

consistency, 123, 127, 183, 194, 201–3, 211

consultant, technical pre-sales, 157

Consultant-as-Seller, 53–54, 56, 58, 60–62

Consultants-as-Sellers, 55, 59, 61, 63

contact, eye, 72, 77, 86, 139

contract, 14, 20, 26, 62, 81–84, 100, 103, 140, 146–47, 157, 170, 195, 210, 229, 236, 270

  cloud transformation, 112

  long-term, 149

  signed, 143, 172

contract signature, 24, 231, 234

  celebrated, 231

contract size, 212, 246

contractual commitments set, 81

contractual obligations, 55, 81

conversation, 13–14, 20, 32–35, 38–39, 47, 51, 61, 66, 68, 72, 80, 86–89, 98–102, 108, 113, 118, 120–21, 123–28, 131, 135, 137, 139, 143, 147–49, 152, 155, 170, 174–78, 187, 191–92, 196, 200, 206, 208–9, 212, 215–16, 220, 223, 237, 276

  direct, 29, 108

  high-stakes sales, 13

  high-trust sales, 29

  strategic, 56, 123–25, 128, 216

  well-structured, 123

conversation shifts, 68, 173

conviction, 7, 21–22, 66, 78, 90, 140, 154–55, 209, 212, 232

cost, 11, 25–26, 33, 39, 43, 67–68, 92, 101, 105, 111, 113, 117–19, 121, 136–38, 142–44, 152, 155, 157, 173–75, 177, 183, 187, 200, 204, 222, 237, 246–47, 251, 269

  operational, 133

cost centers, 118, 120, 210

Cost-Centric Buyers, 5, 173

Cost of Arbitrary Deadlines in Sales, 255

cost savings, 82, 119, 131, 177

cost structure, 104

create momentum, 36, 149, 203

create urgency, 175

credibility, 10, 28, 33, 35–36, 40, 47, 50, 52–53, 62–63, 66, 99, 101, 108, 115, 125–26, 138, 154, 191, 202–3, 222–23, 225, 237

cues, nonverbal, 76–77

culture of ownership, 83–84, 185

customer advocacy, 184–85

customer alignment, long-term, 271
customer commitment, 20, 83
customer conversations, 274
customer engagement, 81, 150, 187, 259
   long-term, 186
customer engagement framework, 270
customer expansion, 185, 252
customer outcomes, 4, 81–82, 211, 229
customer relationships, 58, 62, 96, 147, 183, 186, 232, 255, 257
Customer Risk, 1
customers, 7, 11, 14, 16, 21, 23–26, 31, 40, 46, 50–51, 53–59, 61–63, 65, 69, 78–81, 83–84, 88, 93, 96, 99, 101, 103, 108, 111, 113, 115, 120–21, 123–28, 135, 137–38, 141–43, 147–49, 152–56, 173, 181–84, 186–87, 193–95, 197–202, 204, 206–8, 212, 215–19, 221, 226, 228, 231–32, 235–36, 238–39, 241–42, 248, 250–53, 255–57, 259, 263, 267–70, 272, 275
customer segmentation framework, 269
Customer Segmentation Model, 266, 269
customers experience, 194, 271
customer strategy functions, 62
customer success, 58, 82–83, 183, 185, 201, 231–32, 241, 271, 276
customer success scorecard, 24, 82, 84
customer success teams, 84
customer trusts, 53, 186
customization, 181, 186, 268
customized security frameworks, 270

D

Daniel, 188–89
David, 72–73, 85–87, 199–200
deadlines, 255–59
delays, 10, 28, 37, 39, 43, 89, 118–19, 126–29, 138, 144, 173, 175–77, 190, 256–57
   modeling, 44
deliverables, 33, 81, 84, 147
   scoped, 234
delivery, 21, 25, 50–51, 53–56, 59–61, 63, 103, 140, 143, 178, 182, 185, 193–95, 197–201, 210, 228–29, 232, 234, 236–41, 243–44, 246–47, 250–52, 261, 276
   executive aligning, 266
   long-term, 255
   micromanage, 195
   scoped, 263
delivery alignment, 238
delivery capacity, 243, 256
delivery costs, 236, 256
delivery leaders, 196, 247
delivery leadership, 55
delivery model design, 247
delivery risk, 250
   managing, 60
   on-time, 39

delivery teams, 20, 25, 54, 83, 141, 182–86, 193–94, 231, 242, 246, 249, 251, 256–58, 261

delivery teams burn, 237

delivery team steps, 24

delivery vendor, 114

deployments, 118, 128, 130, 269–70

De-Risk the Decision, 29

Designing Tiered Service Offerings for Scalability, 266, 268

developers, 128, 130, 133–34, 217–19

digital transformation project, 111, 117

discipline, 93–94, 139, 144, 203, 205, 225, 236, 239, 258, 260

  executional, 102

  sales leadership, 237

discounts, 5, 21–22, 67, 137, 139, 141, 146, 174, 222, 240–41, 250, 252, 256–57, 259, 261

downtime, unplanned, 85–87

E

Eli, 232–36

Elise, 72–74

embedding delivery partners, 60

Enablement Framework, 267, 272

enablers, long-term strategic, 218

End of the Conversation, 187, 191

End-to-end partnership model, 199

engagement, 24, 35, 50, 60, 62, 81, 83, 105, 123, 127, 129, 131, 135, 147–48, 150–52, 157, 175, 181–83, 187, 190, 194, 199, 208, 216, 218, 230, 241–42, 267–68, 270, 272

  expansion, 267

  initial, 81, 149

  long-term, 123, 229, 269

  outcome-based, 62

  post-sale, 183, 185

  time-and-materials, 228

engagement history, 218

engagement managers, 55

Engagement Model, 211

  continuous, 271

  hybrid, 198

enterprise, 52, 70, 221, 267–69, 276

enterprise buyers, 10

enterprise customers, 58, 60, 198

enterprise decisions, 37, 70

enterprise IT buyers, 249

enterprise sales leader, 118

enterprise sales process, 27

Evolution of Risk Management, 111

Evolution of Service Sales, 186, 215

execution, 4–5, 7, 13, 25, 33, 35, 44–46, 48, 50, 56, 59–60, 74, 81, 94, 96–97, 143, 156, 178, 182–83, 186, 188–91, 193, 195, 197, 207, 210, 223, 226–27, 233, 238, 244, 253, 267, 276

  bespoke, 247

  credible, 43

  disciplined, 207

  fragments, 210

  go-to-market, 266

scaling, 5, 178
strategic, 220, 223
trusted, 60
executional confidence, 58
execution capacity, 141
execution confidence, 54
execution discipline, 94
execution gap, 47
execution integrity, 259
execution machines, 63
execution matter, 276
Execution Models, 6, 266
execution moments, 154
execution partner, 34, 36, 202–3
execution plans, 32
execution problems, 255
execution readiness, 195
execution risk, 174
execution strategies, 96
Execution to Strategy, 131
Execution wobbles, 63
executive advocacy, 82
executive alignment, 151, 175, 194
executive altitude, 56
executive approval, 65, 246
executive attention shifts, 151
executive battle, 154
Executive Briefing Memo, 155
executive briefs, 211
executive confidence, 276
executive decision-makers, 38
executive defensibility, 37

executive engagement, 57, 151, 175
Executive Lens, 68
executive level, 37, 62
Executive Levers for Scalable Profitability, 6, 245
executive meetings, 196
executive peers, 146
executive perception, 44
executive priorities, 15, 175
executive relationships, 15
executive relevance, 66
executive reviews, 74, 154
executives, 10, 18, 31, 47, 54, 68–69, 71, 89, 91, 93, 148–49, 170, 173, 175, 177, 204, 225, 245–46, 248, 251, 259, 263
senior, 68
skeptical, 71, 220
executive signs, 28
executive sponsor, 40, 117, 142, 152
executive sponsor exposure, 39
executive sponsorship, 30
expansion models, 268
expansions, 62, 82, 147–49, 230–32, 246, 261, 271–72
post-sale, 55
expertise, 9–10, 12, 33, 37, 66, 93, 96, 99, 187, 189–91, 215
consultative sales, 272

F

facial expressions, 76–78
failure, downstream execution, 256

fallback plans, 71, 155
finance teams, 118, 121, 136, 142
financial frameworks, 228
financial impact, 112–13, 137, 174
financial modeling, 121
financial outcomes, 118
Financial Translation Framework, 118
firms, 60, 62–63, 102, 112, 115, 117–18, 136, 181, 185
  first, 112
  scalable service, 187
first conversation, 98, 239
fluency, executional, 53
foundation, 4, 8, 14, 20, 26, 46, 81, 185, 207, 274
frame post-sale success, 210
frameworks, 5–6, 12, 34, 36–37, 39, 47, 82, 93, 95, 125, 155, 178, 181, 187, 189, 207–10, 212–13, 266–67, 271–72, 274
frustrated customers, 183–84
Future of Risk Management, 115
future of service sales, 5–6, 206, 214–15, 219, 224, 260, 267, 271

G

governance, 70, 113–14, 229
  executive-level, 30
growth, 55, 57–58, 61, 68, 135, 150, 179, 181, 186, 206, 232, 237, 245, 247, 249, 266
  long-term, 269
Growth Ceiling, 5, 198
guidance, strategic, 84, 189

guide strategy sessions, 266

H

handoffs, 24, 182, 193, 197, 206
  sales-to-delivery, 266
headcount, 243, 245, 247
health, long-term customer, 231
healthcare providers, 98, 217
Health Insurance Portability and Accountability Act (HIPAA), 100
helping sales teams focus, 269
Hidden Cost of Poor Risk Management, 111
High Cost of Chasing, 6, 255
high-performing services businesses, 247
high revenue, 237
High-Stakes Reality of Services, 9
high-trust sales approach blends, 194
HIPAA (Health Insurance Portability and Accountability Act), 100
hotels, 40–42
human sales professional, 221

I

Ideal Customer Typical Deliverables, 268
Identify and Shift the Buyer's Mindset, 190
implementation, 33, 91, 104, 125, 157, 182, 199, 268, 270
implementation leaders, 198

implementation timelines, 83, 87, 110

improvements, 118–19, 134, 143, 148, 185

inaction, cost of, 37, 67, 152

industry, 57, 69–70, 86, 88, 125–26, 215–17, 269

industry trends, 215–16

infrastructure teams, 129

in-person meetings, 194, 196, 198

integrity, 4, 20–21, 23–26, 69, 203

intentional pursuit strategies, 63

internal teams, 38, 43, 156, 198, 207, 238

Investing in Scalable Service Models, 247

investment, 68, 85–88, 105–6, 108, 118, 120, 131, 133, 138, 143–44, 149, 157, 176, 217

IT operations, 104, 156, 187

IT service management platform, 103

J

Jake, 104–6, 108

joint discovery sessions, 101

Julien, 144–46

K

Kathleen, 32–35

key interfaces, 53–57

Key to Long-Term Customer Engagement, 149

L

language, 11, 29, 37, 53, 56, 67–68, 72, 93–94, 155, 183, 242–43
body, 76–77, 80, 144

language decision-makers, 117, 136

leaders, 39, 41, 51, 62, 115, 120, 185, 187, 190, 206, 210–11, 249, 253
operational, 38, 71
technical, 38

leadership, 33–35, 57, 73, 83, 104, 106–8, 129–31, 133–34, 157, 175–77, 184–86, 198, 228, 231, 245, 276–77
frustrated, 85
market, 272
operational, 209

leadership cares, 131, 175

leadership conversations, 236

leadership level, 108, 132

leadership moment, 14

Leadership Shift, 184

leadership team, 156, 181, 199, 210

Leading Sales Teams, 230

Leading the Next Era of Service Sales, 219

Lisa, 15–16, 18, 105–6

long-term consequences, 174, 257

long-term customer relationships, 228

long-term impact, 174, 185

long-term partnerships, 35, 81, 83–84

long-term sales effectiveness, 255

long-term success, 81, 96, 123, 149, 232, 271
long-term value, 60, 183, 216, 231
Lorna, 232–34
Losing Strategic Value, 5, 181, 185
Losing Trust, 6, 225

M

managed service contracts, 231
managed service relationships, 56
Managed Services Providers (MSPs), 62
managing sales, 256, 258
margin
  contribution, 212, 246, 248
  services organizations track, 248
Margin-aware sales professionals, 238
margin discipline, 6, 246, 249
Margin Mindset, 6, 236
margin point, 249
margin retention, 195, 197
Mastering Body Language & Non-Verbal Sales Cues, 4, 76
Mastering Procurement, 5, 173
measurable outcomes, 184, 187, 197, 271
Meera, 187–89, 191
Meera's team, 190
metrics, financial, 121, 238
Michael, 156–57
mid-market, 267–69
Mike, 15–16, 18

mindset shift, 114, 239
misalignment, 29, 37, 57, 68, 184, 193, 195, 197, 256
Misleading Safety of Revenue Growth, 245
mistakes salespeople, 79, 152
model, 16, 36, 39, 45, 60–61, 63, 93, 114, 119–20, 183, 185, 199, 201, 211, 215, 228, 230, 233, 247, 261, 267, 272
  coownership, 185
  financial, 27
  long-term, 230
  maturity, 207, 267
Models with Two Outcomes, 253
Modern Models, 4, 58
Modern Revenue Recognition Models, 6, 228
moments, 7, 9, 13, 16, 18–21, 24, 34, 50, 76, 85, 93–94, 110, 117, 120, 130, 136–37, 140, 144–45, 170, 174, 187, 191, 193–94, 196, 202, 204, 209, 212, 215, 227, 251, 255, 261, 263–64, 266
  dangerous, 193
  right, 88
momentum, 5, 24, 28, 39, 46, 55, 65, 67, 87, 103, 127, 144, 146, 151–52, 155, 206, 223, 245
  breaks, 57
  losing, 270
  market, 68
  natural, 124
momentum falters, 48
momentum stalls, 150–51

momentum stops, 94

money, 69–70, 94, 107, 113–15, 118, 174, 222

money story, 118–19, 143

MSPs (Managed Services Providers), 62

multilevel influence, 37, 42–43, 46, 96

multiyear agreements, 229, 231

multiyear services engagement, 157

N

Net revenue retention, 212, 230

new reality, 4, 9

New Revenue Recognition Models and Their Impact on Services Sales, 228

Northbeam, 251–52, 254

Northbeam Consulting, 249, 251, 253

O

objections, 209, 221, 226, 263

operating margin, 236, 245, 250, 252

operational disruptions, 112–13

operational inefficiencies, 124, 126, 129, 143, 152, 181, 209

operational overhead, 131, 133

operations leaders, 145, 157

operations leadership, 38

operations teams, 127, 129

optimization, 147–48, 182, 229, 268–70

organizations, 23, 36, 50, 52–53, 55, 57, 67, 96, 98, 155, 181, 184–86, 193–94, 206, 232, 239, 247, 258, 267–68, 270–72

outcome alignment, 200

outcomes, 6, 9, 11, 13, 21–22, 26, 28, 34, 38, 55–56, 58, 61, 81, 88, 90, 99, 101–3, 108, 115, 125, 127, 133, 139, 146, 153, 155–57, 182, 195, 197, 200–202, 206, 210, 212–13, 220, 229, 242, 249, 252, 260, 264, 277

overpromising delivery timelines, 237

ownership, 7, 9, 17–18, 58, 63, 81–83, 100, 113–14, 137, 153, 185, 189–91, 208, 211–12, 238, 263

shared, 68, 194

total cost of, 152, 174

Ownership Framework, 112–13

Owning Customer Risk, 3

P

Path from Strategic Positioning to Execution, 103

patterns, 12, 199, 215–16, 220, 225–26, 255

pillars, 36–43, 45, 93–95, 203–4, 239

Pillars of Service Sales, 4, 93

Pillars of Strategic Partnership, 36

pilot, 54, 133–35, 211

Pilot to Enterprise-Wide Strategy, 133

pipeline, 25, 103, 153, 178, 206, 210, 243, 245, 258–59

well-structured, 258

playbooks, structured sales, 183

post-sale outcomes, 63

post-sales success, 230
post-sale success plan, 184
power, 4, 52–56, 85, 102, 118, 177, 221, 274
Power of Strategic Conversations in Service Sales, 127
Power of Strategic Silence, 138
Prep, managing executive, 16
Pre-sales architects, 53, 61
pressure, 7, 10, 12–13, 23–24, 33, 35–36, 43, 52, 65, 70, 72, 75, 93, 101, 136, 144, 151, 176, 204, 209, 238, 261
pressure buyers, 46
Prevented costly delays, 190
price, 9, 21–22, 29–30, 37, 93, 103, 113–14, 118, 137, 140–41, 143, 145, 152, 156, 173–77, 212, 221, 237–38, 240–41, 252, 256, 260
priorities, 23, 42, 106, 108, 123–24, 127, 175, 256
procurement, 14–15, 52, 67–68, 70–71, 139–40, 142–43, 151–53, 157, 173–77, 222–23, 241, 263
procurement processes, 217, 257
procurement teams, 68, 148, 217
professional risk-carrier, 202
profitability, 6, 236, 249, 251, 256, 259
project deliverables, 82
projected timelines, 72
projects, 23, 28–30, 34, 36, 40–41, 43, 69, 71, 74, 82–83, 100, 117, 136, 140, 146–49, 174, 182, 188–89, 198, 209, 217, 228, 250, 258, 275
project teams, 111, 148
Protecting Margin, 6, 240
providers, 9, 81–84, 98, 100–101, 111, 149, 157, 174, 176, 183, 217, 269
 low-cost, 177
Proving Value Early to Secure Long-Term Success, 149
pursuits, 15, 37, 55, 57, 62–63
pursuit teams, 54, 63, 263
 coached executive, 276

Q

qualification, 99–100, 103, 178, 194, 211
quarter, 102, 174, 178, 182, 202, 206, 228, 233, 235, 240, 248, 255–59
 next, 33, 90, 257–58
quarterly business reviews, 184, 196
questions, 9–10, 16–18, 23, 28, 30, 32, 53, 72, 74, 84, 86–87, 94, 100, 105–6, 111–12, 114–15, 118–22, 126, 130, 132, 137–38, 202, 212, 263, 274
quiet moments, 66

R

Rachel, 72–75
Reading the Signals, 33, 72
realization, 136–37, 143–46, 191
real outcomes, 7, 22, 47
real time, 76, 217, 221–22, 244, 247, 252, 272

recurring revenue, 229, 260
Redefining Sales Metrics and Performance Management, 230
Reframing the Services Strategy, 199
Reigniting Momentum with Strategic Interventions, 151
Repeatable Success, 5, 178
resilience, 5, 68, 202–5
revenue, 114, 152, 184–86, 228–29, 231–32, 236–37, 245, 255–56, 258–59, 272
  milestone-based, 228
revenue growth, 82, 230, 245
revenue recognition, 233–34
Rise of Developers and Software in Sales Strategy, 217
risk, 4, 7, 11, 13, 18, 20, 25, 27–28, 30, 33, 35, 38–39, 43, 47, 50, 53, 56, 59, 61, 63, 66, 69–71, 73, 82, 88–94, 98, 110–16, 127, 129, 133, 137–39, 146, 149, 154–55, 170–71, 174, 177–78, 191, 199, 202–3, 209–13, 215, 225–27, 236, 240, 242, 259, 261, 263–64, 277
  financial, 112
  operational, 69, 152
  potential, 111, 223
  real, 22, 115, 145, 209
  reduced, 117, 136
  scaling, 206
  service sales teams approach, 111
  spot, 226, 247
risk absorption, 38, 46
risk aversion, 89, 91
risk avoidance, 41, 114, 174
Risk-Based Momentum, 37, 42, 44, 46
risk conversations, 171, 211
risk exposure, 14, 121
risk management, 5, 110–11, 115
risk management framework, 112
risk mitigation, 62, 96, 174
risk ownership, 4, 36, 40–41, 94, 115, 227
Risk Ownership Framework, 4, 93
risk signals, 220
ROI, 27, 67, 85, 90, 120, 269
ROI models, 89, 119, 241
Role of Strategic Conversations in Service Sales, 123
Role of the Executive, 248
roles, services sales, 58

S

sales, 3–6, 9–10, 20–21, 27, 51–52, 59–60, 63, 65, 76, 78–79, 83, 87, 89, 110, 113, 124, 126–27, 137, 153, 182–86, 193–95, 197, 199, 201, 208, 215, 218–19, 224, 231, 234, 236, 243–44, 246–47, 253, 256–57, 267, 272, 276
  effective services, 238
  high-performing services, 57
  initial, 183, 186, 216
  product, 53, 212, 256
  senior, 210, 217
  structure services, 259

technical, 14
sales approaches, 10, 269
sales books, 4, 7, 154
sales culture, 231, 251
sales cycles, 53, 101, 181–82, 186, 242, 267, 270
  transactional, 219
sales director, 183–84
sales engagements, 217
sales framework, 208
sales interactions, 76, 127
sales leader building, 266
sales leaders, 114, 117, 121, 128, 136, 195, 230, 232, 255, 258
sales leadership, 276
sales leaders trust, 25
sales manager, 232
Sales Maturity Model, 266–67
sales model, 10, 268
sales motions, 54–55, 62–63
sales organizations, 230
  effective, 257, 259
sales ownership, 58
sales pitches, 217
sales pressures, 255
sales process, 24, 98, 103, 115, 193, 209, 257, 267, 271
sales professionals, 65, 124, 126–27, 147, 149, 183, 185, 218, 221, 228, 237
  effective, 123, 125
  elite, 76
  replacing, 215–16

sales rep, 6, 216, 230, 232, 250
Sales Service, 272
Sales Shift, 200
sales strategies, 260, 269
sales success, 259
sales tactics, 101, 257
sales teams, 14–15, 100, 110–11, 115, 117, 119, 136, 147, 182–86, 200, 215–16, 218, 220, 222, 229–31, 236, 240, 246, 255–56, 258, 267, 269, 271
  best, 103, 218
  five-person, 267
  less-experienced, 187
sales teams risk, 270
sales teams stop, 259
sales timeline, 256
sales tools, 244
scale service sales, 185–86
scaling, 133–34, 149, 179, 181, 186, 210–11, 217, 267
scaling service sales, 5, 181, 183–85
scaling value, 94
Scaling with Structure, 267, 271
scope, 11, 23–24, 33, 36, 39, 53–55, 58, 60–61, 63, 81, 83, 129, 135, 141, 182, 188, 201, 230, 236–38, 241–43, 250, 252, 264
Scope & Delivery Strategy, 6, 240
scope creep, 242
scope execution, 38
scope risk, 248
Seamless Engagement Framework,

266, 270

Seconds of Silence, 5, 144

sellers, 10, 14, 21, 23, 25, 36–38, 51, 66, 69–71, 74, 90–93, 98–99, 102, 137–39, 142–47, 156, 188, 196, 202–3, 208–11, 213, 220–23, 225–27, 231–32, 235, 238–39, 242–44, 250–53, 256–58, 260

   best, 68, 137, 209, 225

   high-pressure, 264

   human, 222–23

   margin-aware, 238

   seasoned, 21, 221

selling services, 15, 20, 28, 31, 50, 215, 264

Selling to the Real Decision-Maker, 31, 92

senior leaders, 204, 276

service contract, 157

service delivery, 81

service delivery expectations, 229

service engagement, 256

   high-trust, 36

service leaders, 84

service leaders position, 84

Service Level Agreements (SLAs), 41, 62, 82

Service Managers, 55–56, 58, 61–63, 178

service models, 271

service offerings, 56, 268

   managed, 228

service organizations, 50, 83, 115, 198, 207, 249

service professionals, 84

service providers, 9–11, 81–82, 84, 100, 111, 114, 123–24, 149, 174, 184, 186, 215, 217, 269

   transactional, 81, 181

service providers move, 84

service providers position, 103

service quality, long-term, 174

services, 4, 7, 9–10, 22, 25, 32–33, 35, 39, 45, 50, 52–53, 56, 58–63, 67, 69, 82, 89, 101, 103, 123–24, 128, 152–53, 156–57, 173–75, 182–84, 187, 194, 198–99, 201, 206, 210, 212, 216–18, 228–30, 232, 234, 236, 240–42, 245, 250–51, 253, 256, 261, 268, 270, 276

   advisory, 83, 268, 270

   buy, 88, 108, 206

   complex, 28, 121

   discounted, 256

   financial, 70, 217

   high-stakes, 21

   managed, 157, 229, 233–34, 268

   position, 147, 218

   professional, 7, 50, 55, 181

service sales, 4, 9–10, 14, 20, 26–27, 36, 50–53, 65, 94, 98–99, 102, 113, 117, 120, 123, 136–37, 139, 144, 151, 181, 186, 195, 198, 205, 210, 212, 215–16, 220, 226, 255–58, 261, 268, 271–72, 276

   complex, 27

   foundation of, 93, 96

   high-stakes, 19, 140

modern, 14, 98, 144
slowed, 216
stagnating, 184
Service Sales Accelerator, 274, 276
service sales conversations, 125
service sales execution, 272
Service Sales Maturity Model, 267
Service sales organizations, 267
service sales performance, 212
service sales professionals, 127, 186, 217
service sales teams, 217–18, 229, 232
services business, 237–38, 245, 249
services deal, scoped, 257
Service Seller Archetypes, 4, 52
service sellers, 5, 31, 72, 150, 173, 176, 194, 202, 206, 235, 263, 274
  biggest mistake, 177
  disciplined, 178
services engagements, 15, 257
services leader, 182
services margin, 200
services market, 249
services revenue, 59
services sales leaders, 228
services sales models, 228
services salespeople, 54
services team positioning, 38
services teams, 198, 229
service tiers, 267–68
service timelines, 198
session, 101, 127, 129–30, 210

shared framework, 183, 186
Shift from Vendor to Strategic Partner, 11
shifting business goals, 81
shifting the conversation, 131, 173
Shifting the Conversation from Cost to Value, 174
Short in Service Sales, 221
Signal Confidence, 21, 78
signal engagement, 79
signals, 46, 52, 56, 67–68, 72, 76, 78, 85, 90, 94, 101, 104, 131, 137, 139–40, 146, 170–71, 194, 197, 221–22, 226, 257, 263
silence, 16, 21, 30, 71, 73, 86, 93–94, 110, 138–39, 143–46, 154, 170, 189, 202–3, 225–27, 263–65, 277
Silent Advantage, 4, 76
skilled procurement professionals, 139
SLAs (Service Level Agreements), 41, 62, 82
slides, 12–13, 21, 32, 47, 65, 74, 85, 94, 101, 138, 144, 238, 261, 263
Small Teams to Enterprise Scalability, 266–67
social proof, 101–2, 123–24, 126–27
sponsor, 65, 143, 263
stakeholder engagement, 199
stall momentum, 54
story, 5, 7, 24, 44, 46, 66, 85–88, 93–95, 98, 102, 117, 144, 154–56, 193, 202–3, 222
Strategic, 199, 268–69

long-term, 149
Strategic Advantage, 5, 110
Strategic Alignment, 4, 49
strategic assets, 210–11
strategic conversations drive decisions, 127
strategic empathy, 69, 207, 261
　deploying, 65
strategic imperatives, 39, 68
strategic partners, 9, 11, 81–82, 114, 135, 147, 156
Strategic Partnership Framework, 4, 36, 45
strategic positioning, 5, 98, 100
strategic priorities, 133, 152, 176
Strategic Risk Discussion, 5
Strategic Service Sales Mindset, 4, 8
Strategic Trust Building, 36, 40, 43, 46
strategic value, 181–82, 184, 186–87, 196
Strategist roles, 62
strategists guide positioning, 60
strategy
　cloud, 156–57
　deliberate expansion, 149
　go-to-market, 276
　long-term, 190
　prevention, 113
　risk-mitigation, 101
strategy session, 10, 15
strategy slides, 260
structure, 12, 37, 39, 51, 63, 93, 127, 181, 199, 201, 211, 215, 228, 231, 235–37, 240, 242, 244, 255, 266, 268
　compensation, 229–30
structured engagement frameworks, 271
structured scoping teams, 63
structure engagements, 266
Structuring Conversations, 148
Structuring Conversations for Maximum Impact, 125
success, 4, 9, 11, 14, 18, 20, 24, 37, 50, 57, 60, 69, 71, 81–84, 87, 96–97, 99–100, 102, 123–24, 127–28, 132–33, 135, 148, 153, 157, 170, 181, 184, 189, 191, 195, 202, 219–20, 230, 239, 242
success in service sales, 81, 84, 207
success stories, 87–88, 125
supply chain systems, 83
support execution, 227
sustainable growth, 57, 184, 212
Sustainable Service Sales, 5, 208

T

tactical empathy, 71, 74
Tactical Empathy in Action, 4, 72
TCV (total contract value), 228, 232
teams, 9, 11–12, 14, 16–19, 21, 29–35, 39–43, 46–47, 50–51, 54–57, 60–61, 84, 87–88, 101, 104, 112, 114, 119–21, 124, 126–29, 133–34, 138, 144, 148–49, 157, 170, 181–82, 185, 187–91, 195, 197–201, 204, 208, 210–12, 230, 232, 236–38, 241–43, 245–48, 258,

261, 263, 271
  decision-making, 176
  engineering, 188, 218
  executive, 9, 28, 174
  marketing, 12
team sport, 50, 244
technical benefits, 118, 121
technical buyers, 142, 218
technical stakeholders, 54, 217
technical teams, 15, 131
technology services, 81, 103, 111
ticket resolution times, 105, 107
timeline credibility, 69
timelines, 23, 30, 69, 75, 81, 100–102, 121, 141, 176–77, 188, 193, 195, 199, 233–34, 242
timelines shift, 30
tools, 6, 39, 101, 138, 155, 213, 219–20, 223–25, 227, 241, 255, 260, 266–67, 274
  profitability modeling, 247
total contract value (TCV), 228, 232
track revenue growth, 229
Train sales teams, 84
transformation, 16, 22, 60–61, 67, 81, 84, 88, 98, 128, 135–36, 156, 183–84, 208, 232, 245, 268–69
  customer service, 118
  digital, 83, 215, 268
transformation engagements, 232, 243
transformation project, 142
Translation, 90–92
trust, 4, 7, 10, 14–15, 19–20, 25–27, 31–36, 38–40, 46–47, 50, 54–55, 58–60, 62–64, 66–67, 73, 76–77, 88, 93–94, 96, 100, 103, 110, 114, 116, 128, 137, 142, 144, 149, 170, 178, 194–97, 200, 207–8, 213, 220, 222, 225, 227, 232, 237–39, 243, 246, 256–57, 261, 263–64, 266–67, 272, 276
  erode, 256
  foundation of, 123, 194
  lens of, 70, 211
Trust-Accelerating Power of In-Person Moments, 196
trusted advisors, 23, 127
trusted partner, 147, 223
Trusted Partner Beyond the Sale, 84
trust gaps, 58, 71
trust is built, 34, 38, 59, 66, 94, 100, 178, 223
trust ownership, 45
trust shifts, 102
Trust to Growth, 200
Turning Buyer Hesitation, 4, 89
Turning Conversations, 5, 123
Turning Trust, 4, 96

U

Understanding Customer Behavior & Strategic Empathy in Service Sales, 4, 65
unpredictable delivery timelines, 181

V

Value-Added Resellers (VARs), 61

value conversations, 241, 252

value realization, 16, 59, 234

Value Translation, 5, 36, 41, 43; 46, 117

VARs (Value-Added Resellers), 61

vendors, 9, 11, 14–15, 17, 30, 35, 40, 42, 66, 69, 71, 73, 82, 84, 94, 98, 112, 125, 127, 135, 139, 141, 147, 149, 157, 187, 209, 218

vision, 31, 56, 60, 68, 157, 193, 222

   long-term, 5, 147, 149

voice tone, 77–78

VP, 106–8, 125, 144, 188, 198, 250, 253

VP of sales, 118, 218, 252

W

Well-Timed Success Story, 4, 85

William values time, 277

winning service sales, 155

[Created with **TExtract** / www.TExtract.com]

William Anderson

Look for more books from Winged Hussar Publishing, LLC and Iron Srategy Press – E-books, paperbacks and Limited-Edition hardcovers. The best in history, science fiction and fantasy at:

https://www.whpsupplyroom.com

or follow us on Facebook and Instagram at:

Winged Hussar Publishing LLC

Or on twitter at:

WingHusPubLLC

For information and upcoming publications